KIRKCALDY HARBOUR

An Illustrated History

CAROL McNEILL

AMBERLEY

Acknowledgements

My thanks go to: Carr's Hutchison's Mill, Dysart Trust, Iain Flett, Jim Fraser, Owen Harrison, John Jack, Bob Kilgour, Kirkcaldy Boat Club, Kirkcaldy Civic Society, Kirkcaldy Galleries, the Mackenzie family, Pearl McLachlan, Kenny Murdoch, Tom Mutch, Scottish Historic Buildings Trust, Rena Stewart, Don Swanson, Paul Zander, and the staff of the Local and Family History Department of Kirkcaldy Galleries.

This book is dedicated to the memory of local historian John Y. Lockhart, who knew and loved every old stone on Kirkcaldy harbour.

First published 2018

Amberley Publishing
The Hill, Stroud,
Gloucestershire, GL5 4EP

www.amberley-books.com

ISBN: 978 1 4456 7624 1 (print)
ISBN: 978 1 4456 7625 8 (ebook)

British Library Cataloguing in Publication Data.
A catalogue record for this book is available from the British Library.

Typeset in 10pt on 13pt Celeste.
Origination by Amberley Publishing.
Printed in the UK.

Contents

CHAPTER 1

Early Days

Standing on the old, worn stones of Kirkcaldy harbour today, it's almost impossible to imagine the sight in 1536 when King James V of Scotland and a fleet of seven magnificent ships with their billowing sails left from Kirkcaldy harbour for France to claim a French princess as his bride.

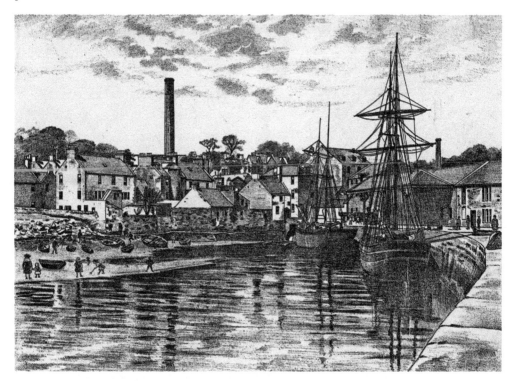

An early sketch of Kirkcaldy harbour. (Kirkcaldy Galleries)

One of the terms of the Auld Alliance, made in the Treaty of Rouen between Scotland and France, was that a Scottish monarch had to marry a French princess to help cement the agreement. James originally intended to make the voyage to France in July of that year, setting out from Leith and going around the north and west coasts of Scotland to avoid being stopped by Henry VIII's ships. However, a severe storm scattered the ships and he had to turn back, but James was determined to carry on, first going to an Edinburgh shrine to pray for a better voyage. He set sail eventually from Kirkcaldy on 1 September with six ships and escorted by 500 soldiers as well as the earls of Arran, Argyll and Rothes and Sir James Kirkaldy of Grange, his Lord High Treasurer, and arrived at Dieppe on 9 September.

James's choice of bride was Madeleine de Valois, a sixteen-year-old French princess who was already in very frail health, having contracted tuberculosis. Despite the wishes of her father François I of France, who was understandably worried about her fragile condition, Madeleine married James in Notre Dame on 1 January 1537 and the couple moved to Scotland, where sadly her health deteriorated rapidly. Poor young Madeleine: a mere pawn in the diplomatic game. She died on 9 July 1537 after a marriage which only lasted for a few months, with a stay in Scotland of only seven weeks. James lost little time and a year later he married again, to the widowed Mary of Guise, who in due course gave birth to Mary, Queen of Scots. Perhaps King James' redeeming role in the whole sorry tale was that he himself had arranged that when he died (which occurred a few days after the birth of his daughter Mary), he chose to be buried beside Madeleine.

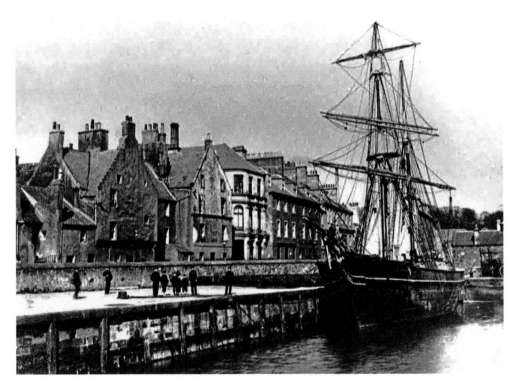

A fine sailing ship is pictured anchored in the dock, probably around 1890, opposite the 'Auld Hoose' (now Sailors Walk). (Kirkcaldy Galleries)

With the town situated on the banks of the Firth of Forth, early merchants and seafarers used the harbour to bring in their goods and raw materials while local manufacturers found it a quick and convenient place to distribute their products both within Britain and very much further afield.

Early Kirkcaldy Town Council harbour records make interesting reading today and give many instances to show what an important and thriving port it was in the sixteenth century. One of the earliest records was in 1505, quoting: 'Wages to John Merchamstoun to seek mariners against the King passing to the Isle of May, 14/-, and 20 mariners brought from Fife: three weeks wages, £10.' In 1567, four haven masters were appointed and given the powers to seize the goods of any skipper who dumped his ballast in the harbour and left it there for 'longer than the space of a tide'. The ballast would be heavy stones, very often flint, and remnants of flint are still being washed up near the harbours throughout Fife. The haven masters were unpaid burgh bailies who had their own non-maritime businesses to attend to; they formed a co-operative group where they took it in turns to go down to the harbour to try to keep it clear and in good order for the benefit of the skippers.

The royal association continued: in 1585 the Council received authority from James VI to fit out two ships to punish English pirates who had attacked a ship owned by a local burgess; some years later it was arranged that eighty carts would attend at Kirkcaldy to lift and remove his Majesty's wardrobe and belongings to Falkland Palace. No travelling light for royalty in those days.

Also recorded is a command from Charles I's Privy Council, which summoned twelve skippers from Pittenweem, twenty-two from Kirkcaldy, eighteen from Leith and five from Dundee to build a lighthouse on the Isle of May. This was erected in 1635 and was a very

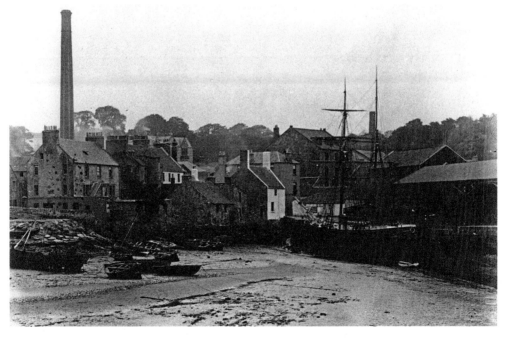

The Harbour Head in 1896 with a sailing ship in the old trinket. (Kirkcaldy Galleries)

primitive structure that consisted of a stone box which burned coal to serve as a light: three men were employed to keep the fire burning all year round, using up to about 400 tons of coal a year. Tragedy struck in 1790 when the lighthouse keeper's entire family were suffocated by fumes, apart from a baby daughter who was found alive three days later.

During the early years of the seventeenth century, James Wemyss gave William Williamson (merchant and skipper of the *Johne* of Kirkcaldy) 1,000 merks to sail with her to Denmark. David Touche, a Kirkcaldy burgess, bought a barque-load of peas from an Englishman in a raid on Kirkcaldy; he sold part of the cargo in Dysart and the rest in Kirkcaldy, much to the annoyance of the town's bailies, who put him in the Tolbooth and fined him £40.

There seems to have been a continuing conflict of loyalties between Scotland and Holland – at times in bitter dispute, and at other times trading peacefully. In 1608 the old records show: 'James Staig, master of the good ship *Hert* of Kirkcaldy bound for Lisbon, was taken by a man-of-war of Holland. The said ship spoiled of her best anchor and tow, victuals, 60 barrels of wheat, three barrels tallow, three barrels salmon, two barrels beef and 300 lbs of linen yarn.' By 1640 however, the export trade in coal and staple wares to Holland was shared by Kirkcaldy and Dysart vessels. Nine years later, the *Elizabeth* from Kirkcaldy sailed to Holland with four Parliamentary Commissioners (the Earl of Cassias, George Winrame of Liberton, Alexander Brodie of Brodie and Alexander Jeffrey, who was Provost of Aberdeen), although the purpose of their representation was not made clear in the records. Captain Myles from Kirkcaldy went out as a privateer against the Dutch in 1666, but twenty years later Provost James Oswald had a vessel trading to Holland, probably with coal and salt. It brought back a variety of goods – slates, tiles, linen yarn

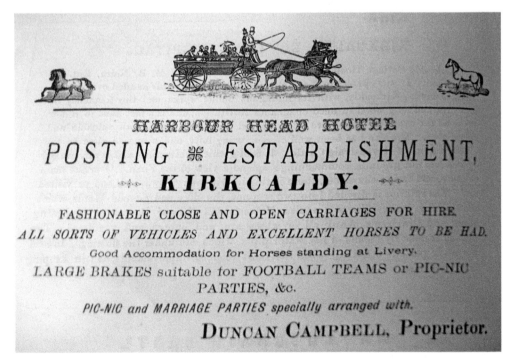

Duncan Campbell owned a hotel at the Harbour Head, providing both transport and provisions.

and dyes – to sell on his own behalf. In 1669 a Dutch fleet appeared in the Forth and fired shots at Burntisland, and two months later the same fleet entered the Thames and burned several English ships.

Imports came in from south of the border too: beer was brought from England on the *James* of Kirkcaldy and the ship *The Grace of God*, which brought ten barrels, and the *Gift of God*, which had nine barrels of beer, with the orders that the beer was not to be sold dearer than 18 pence (Scots) the pint.

The *James* under Captain Robert Masterton carried coal to Holland along with three other local ships, all returning with a cargo of arms and ammunition for the Scottish armies at Newcastle and Ireland in 1643. The cargo was a heavy one: 6,000 muskets, 6,000 bandoliers, 4,000 pikes, 10,000 swords and 10,000 sword belts. The ship was seized at Tynemouth and taken to London, where she was kept for a month. Two other ships along with the *James* carried coal to Leith for the use of the Scottish army in Ireland.

When Charles I was executed in 1649 and Charles II was proclaimed King of Scotland, a deputation sailed from Kirkcaldy in John Gillespie's ship to see him, but returned unsatisfied; in the following year Cromwell visited the town. The importance of Kirkcaldy harbour was reinforced in 1650. The Marquis of Montrose – who initially led the Covenanters against the Royalists in the First Bishops' War in 1639 but later changed sides to support King Charles – was charged with treason and taken prisoner after his last battle. He was put aboard a ship at Kirkcaldy on 18 May 1650 and sailed to Leith on the Saturday: he was tried in Edinburgh on Monday and executed the next day.

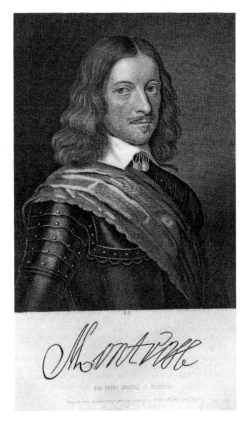

James Graham, 1st Marquis of Montrose, was taken from Kirkcaldy in May 1650 and was executed in Edinburgh for treason.

Two years later General Monk stormed and captured Dundee and obtained 'great treasures belonging to Kirkcaldy which had been sent there for safety'. In the same year, King Charles passed through Kirkcaldy on his way from Burntisland to Wemyss.

Although there were several records made in the seventeenth and eighteenth centuries giving the number of ships belonging to Kirkcaldy, these gave a misleading impression of the town's prosperity at the time: Kirkcaldy was designated Registration Port for Customs purposes for all ports between Aberdour, Leven and Crail. In the 1880s Kirkcaldy made its mark on most of the Fife fishing boats when it became a Port of Registry, meaning that vessels had to carry the KY prefix before their registration number, a practice which still continues today.

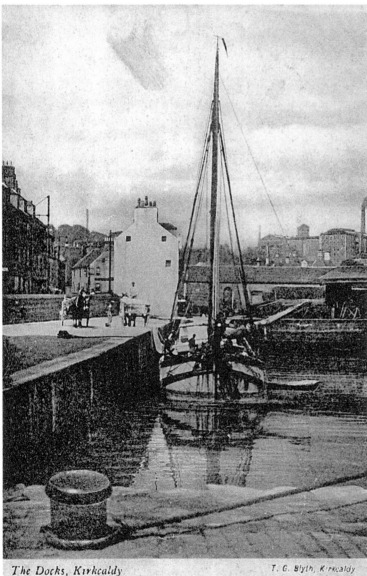

The Docks, Kirkcaldy

T. G. Blyth, Kirkcaldy

Another view of Kirkcaldy docks with horse-drawn carts on the quayside and factory chimneys in the background.

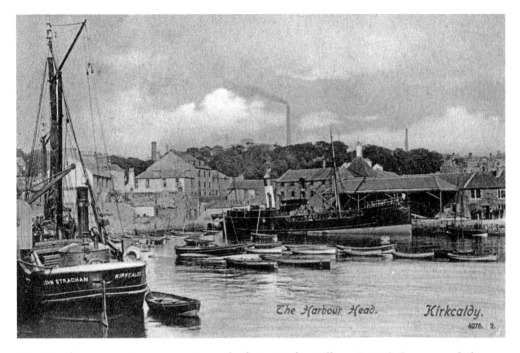

John Strachan was an iron screw steamer built in 1885 by William Swan & Company of Glasgow for the Kirkcaldy, Leith & Glasgow Steam Packet Company.

There were other important and stirring events carefully noted in the seventeenth-century records, including the fact that a Kirkcaldy vessel foundered as it was bringing back to Scotland the old National Records, and that the records were lost. Kirkcaldy was required to send more men to the Navy and to make a contribution to the repair of Burntisland harbour; the town was now named as the Sixth Burgh in Scotland and had to contribute one-fortieth of the total national tax.

The harbour was still featuring in national history near the end of the century. The records said: 'A party of Kirkcaldy men pursue the Earl of Perth as he attempts to escape in a Burntisland ship; capture him near the Bass Rock, bring him back to Kirkcaldy and lodge him in the Tolbooth [then occupying the site of the National Bank] guarded by 300 men. He was then sent by sea with an escort of 200 men to Lord Mar at Alloa. The Highlanders threatened reprisals for this and a guard of 300 men was kept up for four months until danger is past.'

It is also recorded that the Company of Scotland (a Scottish mercantile trading initiative to promote overseas trade) shipped on board the *Isabel* of Kirkcaldy a cargo for Africa consisting of trading goods such as guinea basins, guinea jugs of pewter, coloured beads, copper bars, brass pans, arm rings and bells. Kirkcaldy was then listed by Customs as the fourth port in Scotland.

When the ill-fated Darien Scheme was started up by Scots-born William Paterson in July 1698 to provide a wider market for Scottish merchants, Kirkcaldy ships were among the first to go. The Council minutes recorded that the Company of Scotland had two ships built at Hamburg, the *St Andrew* and the *Caledonia*, which were sent to Kirkcaldy in December to winter there in readiness to sail in July as part of the first Darien Fleet.

11

The scheme, paid for by public subscription, set up a Scottish colony on the Isthmus of Panama to get round the restrictions that meant only English traders could take advantage of trading under the English Navigation Acts.

Although the scheme started out well, with a fort built and friendly connections made with the native inhabitants, the success did not last long. A series of setbacks and disasters occurred: provisions ran out after a supply ship from Scotland was wrecked and the new settlers, who were unaccustomed to the hot weather, contracted tropical diseases. Eventually many of the colonists died and although a second expedition set out on the following year, it too ended in disaster. It was estimated that out of around 2,400 Scottish colonists who took part in the two expeditions, only about fifty survived the whole disastrous plan which had seemed so promising in the beginning.

One historical event that would have never been forgotten by those who witnessed it at the time was when John Paul Jones sailed three of his American warships from Leith to Kirkcaldy, causing great alarm. The Revd Shirra, the first minister of what is now Linktown Church, on being told of the threat from the ships, prayed that the wind would change and

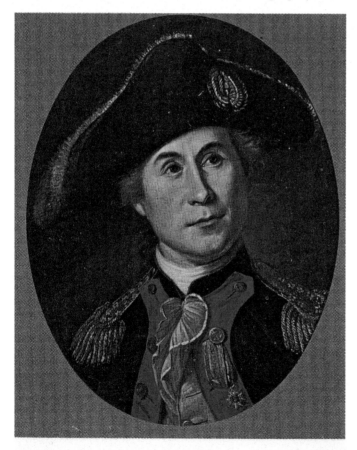

JOHN PAUL JONES

John Paul Jones was born in Scotland and went on to found the American navy.

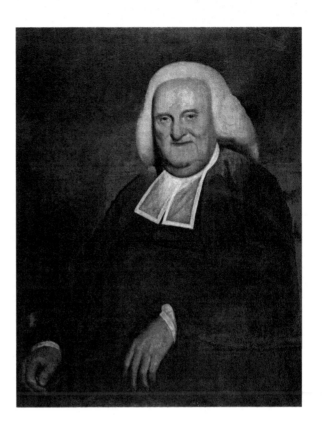

When Paul Jones' ships appeared in the Forth, the Revd John Shirra successfully prayed that the wind would change. (Kirkcaldy Galleries)

that the ships would be blown out of the Forth and away from the Fife coast. An extract from the old Minute Book of the Burgh of Kirkcaldy (1582–1792) recounted an eyewitness account of the event in 1782:

> It was during this time that Paul Jones – who was a roving vagabond, was he not – sailed up the Firth of Forth with three vessels for the purpose of burning the ships at Leith. His visit cause the utmost consternation: Kirkcaldy and Pathhead yard heads were filled with spectators who expected him to land on either Kirkcaldy of Pathhead sands.
>
> The ships which local sailors described as Dutch built were so near the shore that the folks on Pathhead Braes could discern the red shirts of those on board. The ships were described to us by another person who witnessed them not just sailing but 'tumbling down'.
>
> The story is told in different ways but we have never seen it correctly in print, and being so celebrated it may be worth telling correctly. One version is that Mr Shirra knelt down on Pathhead sands and prayed: 'Lord, if they be enemies, put a hook in their nose and a bridle in their jaws, and tak' them back to whaur they came frae.' Another would almost ignore the prayer, merely stating that Mr Shirra said to one of his friends that the Lord with the wind could easily blow him out of the Forth. The first version is the most correct but the place and name is not correctly given. The following was stated by a most respectable person who was present:
>
> Mr Shirra – who has been described as 'a big tall man with a big wig' – came out of his house to the foot of his garden for the purpose apparently of taking a walk. Seeing such

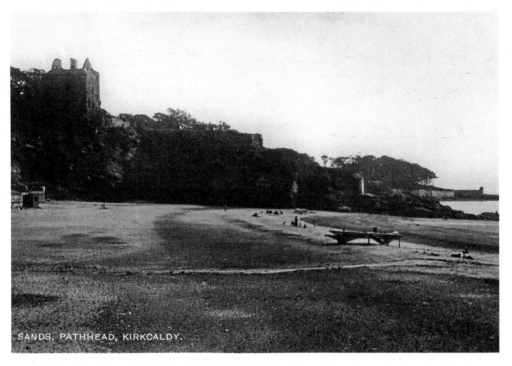

SANDS, PATHHEAD, KIRKCALDY.

Pathhead Sands, near where the Revd Shirra successfully prayed for deliverance from Paul Jones' ships.

a number of people including some boys, amongst whom was our informant, he gathered them together and placed his back against the wall of his garden, took off his hat and prayed that Jones might be drawn away.

There can be no doubt that Mr Shirra prayed against Paul Jones, and no doubt that the pirate was driven down the Forth by a strong west wind. None of the persons present could state the exact time between the prayer and the strong wind, but it could not have been long otherwise the prayer would not be so well remembered. Many people at the time believed it was answered by a direct intervention by Providence.

The Minutes added a mischievous sideline: 'Numbers of Pathhead folk openly buried in their gardens their valuables such as pewter pots, plates etc, but many of them never got them back – there being other and nearer vagabonds than Paul Jones.'

The harbour was still a busy place in 1795 when that year's *Statistical Account* recorded that shipping in Kirkcaldy consisted of twenty-six square-rigged vessels, one sloop and two ferryboats, employing 225 men to navigate them.

In the mid-eighteenth century, one Kirkcaldy man found himself caught up in one of the wars against France. Alexander Williamson's exploits were documented later by his son Thomas in a unique memoir written in 1873:

When my father was at sea he witnessed many a strange plight, what with the Press Gangs carrying off sailors and putting them by force on board the ships of war and the convoys that used to congregate at Leith, Cork and other places.

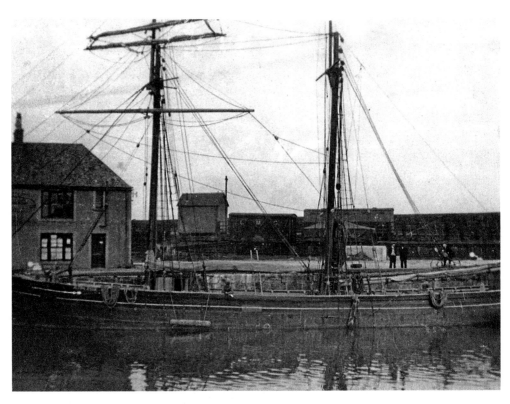

This image of a sailing ship in Kirkcaldy harbour is dated around 1922, when sail was still popular.

The ships of war were bringing in French prisoners, and there were French and American privateers [glorified pirates sponsored by their governments which took a share of the cargoes from the ships which were looted]. The constant danger of captains at sea made a sailor's life at that period a time of peril and excitement.

The Press Gang once carried Williamson off in their boat to Leith and he was put on board a frigate lying in Leith Roads getting manned. A clever fishwife from Fife who used to come with her fish in her creel to Kirkcaldy had heard he was 'pressed'. She set off in a boat with her fish to Leith, went on board the frigate and managed by exchanging part of her dress, and dressing him up with it, got him smuggled into her boat and got him safely away. A noble deed by the fisher woman. She knew his people and probably they asked her to try to get him off. It was a dreadful thing to be forced to serve for three days on board of a Man of War, amid such fighting.

I found my father's name mentioned in an old Edinburgh Almanac of 1813 as one of the 'Sailor Councillors' in the Kirkcaldy list of Magistrates at that time, when Walter Fergus was Provost. At the King's Birthday they were very loyal; they all met opposite the old jail and drank his health and then threw their glasses behind them to the crowd.

Presumably the glasses had been well drained first.

It would seem at that time several Town Council members were drawn from the seafaring community, understandably when the revenue from the harbour trade was one

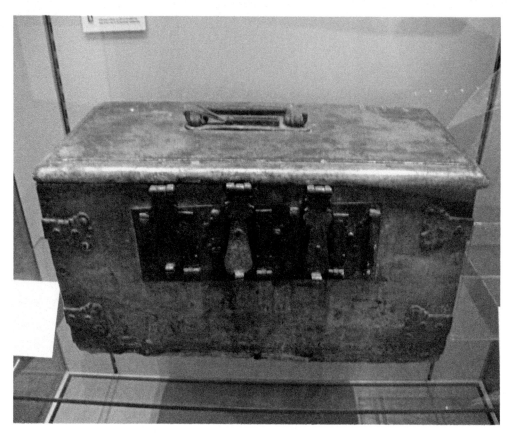

The Prime Gilt Box of Kirkcaldy is on display in Kirkcaldy Galleries.

of the principal sources of Kirkcaldy's income. Presumably these Sailor Councillors looked out for the welfare of the seamen and their families, and may well have administered the revenue from Kirkcaldy's Prime Gilt Box (sometimes referred to then as the Prime Guild Box or the 'puir folks' box), which has been preserved and is on display in Kirkcaldy Galleries. This large and sturdy box dates back to 1591 and belonged to the Prime Gilt Society, which was made up of shipmasters and mariners; it was described as being used 'for relief of their number who may fall into distress'. It raised money through regular payments from those who used the harbour: owners were to pay 6s 8d per year and sailors 2d per voyage once they had come back home. The Society used the money in various ways to help the local poor families.

The box was fitted with three locks, and to ensure against fraud each lock had to be opened with a key held by separate Society members. Old records show that David Law kept possession of the box, James Littlejohn had the records of payment and Thomas Lamb, Alexander Law and David Low each held a key.

Thomson's Directory of 1835 listed no fewer than thirty-three ships 'belonging to the port of Kirkcaldy'. These included *Charles Forbes, Diana, George, Isabella, Marjory, Regalia, Sisters, Union Progress* and the touchingly named *Lovely Maria*. These ships, as well as five whalers, belonged to the well-to-do shipowners and merchants of the burgh, including Beveridge, Dougal, Jamieson, Johnston and Oliphant.

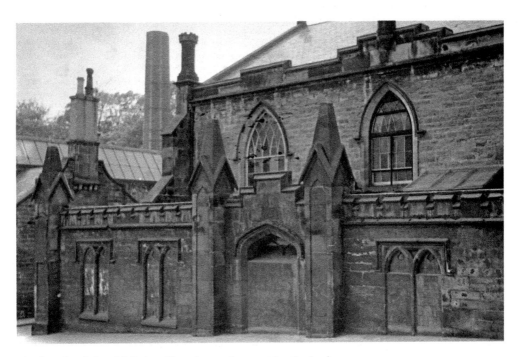

The facade of the old Union Church stands opposite the harbour.

By the 1870s ships including the brig *Triad*, the brig *George Ann* (built by James Brown & Co. in their nearby Rose Street yard) and the barques *Falcon* and *Koh-in-oor* were all owned by Swan Brothers. They were used for the flax trade in summer, and in winter went to the West Indies, returning to Greenock with cargoes of sugar. The sugar trade was taken up by a large number of sailing vessels and one of the fastest voyages ever made was by the barque *Lothrie* (built in the nearby Dysart yard by John Watt) in the record time of four weeks. *Koh-in-oor* was later withdrawn from the flax trade and was completely rebuilt, lengthened and given a new mast at the Dysart yard, and afterwards took part in the Chilean trade, carrying around 700 tons of cargo.

The harbour was of course also used for passenger transport: the early ferry boats were sailing ships before the age of steam, sailing from Kirkcaldy harbour to Newhaven or Leith. By the 1840s, steam boats took the place of sail, with a tax of 2*d* imposed on each passage made. Two of the rival steamers were in such fierce competition that the fares were reduced to sixpence per journey and later dropped further, hitting rock bottom at one penny per trip. It was so cheap that it was quite common for the town's weavers to stop work and have a day's pleasure trip to Leith and back. It usually ended with one rival retiring before he was completely ruined. The ferry trade ended after 1850 when the railway company opened the Granton and Burntisland service.

Andrew Beveridge, in his memories collected by local historian John Lockhart in the early 1900s, recalled:

Before the railway came in 1844, there were passenger steamers for Leith. One was the *Queen* and the rival boat was the *Ben Ledi* – this caused two factions amongst us boys which sometimes brought on fisticuffs. The rivalry between the steamers led to the

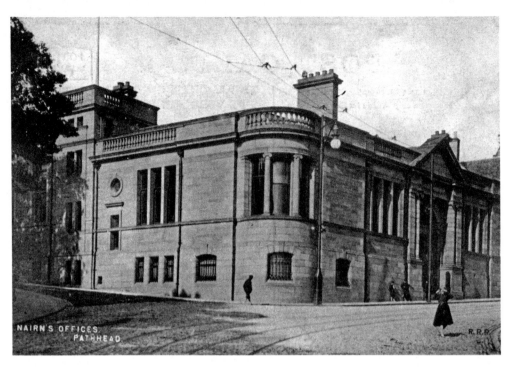

Michael Nairn's offices at the head of the Path.

reductions of fares – you could get to Leith for a penny – but this didn't last long as the *Ben Ledi* had to give up, which was a great victory for the *Queen* supporters. It was always a source of great amusement to see the landing of the passengers. The *Queen* men had hurlies which were taken down when the tide was out and passengers could get ashore dry shod; but the *Ben Ledi* didn't have these so their passengers, among them possibly a fat wife, had to be carried ashore on some little ferryman's back.

There used to be a cheap steam boat trip to Stirling, always largely patronised. One which I attended was met on the return passage near Inch Colm with a very heavy sea from the east, and being nearly 10pm the Captain said he could not take them to Kirkcaldy and would go to Granton. My father, being an old seaman, came to the rescue and said he would pilot the vessel to Burntisland which was done. A special tram was made up to take us back to Kirkcaldy although many took the road for it.

Shortly after the main railway line was built, the stir was again kept up by a branch railway to the harbour and the building of the sea walls on the east side of the harbour. From this time onwards Pathhead [then a separate burgh from Kirkcaldy] began to take on a new life with Nairn's factory, new steam loom factories etc. It has swollen to its present dimensions so that if anyone were to look back seventy years, they would not recognise their old quarters.

As early as 1824, the Leith & Kirkcaldy Shipping Company had premises on the pier, and by the end of the nineteenth century there were two shipping businesses with premises on the harbour itself. The Kirkcaldy, Leith & Glasgow Steam Packet Company Ltd ran daily sailings to Leith and to Glasgow 'as required'; and the SS *Abden* from the London &

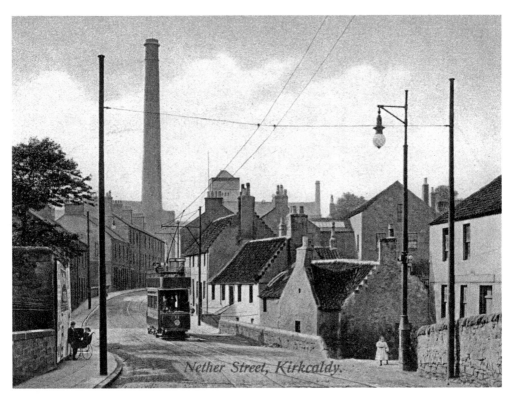

Nether Street in Pathhead.

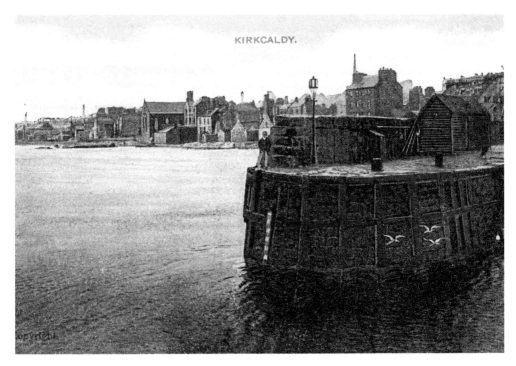

The 'Wee Pier' was a popular anchorage for small boats and ships. (Kirkcaldy Civic Society)

Kirkcaldy Shipping Company had regular sailings every week. In 1928, the Dundee, Perth & London Shipping Company took over the local sailings between Leith and Kirkcaldy, taking linoleum products to Leith and bringing back Danish dairy products in a ship popularly known then as 'the bacon and egg boat'.

By 1936 the same company was advertising services from Kirkcaldy to Leith every Monday and Thursday, and from Leith to Kirkcaldy every Tuesday and Friday. This company also ran regular weekly sailings from Kirkcaldy to Hull, Newcastle, Portsmouth and Southampton; they were also agents for the Coastline group and had regular weekly sailings with cargo vessels to Aberdeen, Bristol, Cardiff, Falmouth, Manchester, Plymouth and Portsmouth, with fortnightly sailings to Stornoway.

Kirkcaldy was also a popular venue for summer cruises: in 1884 for instance, *Carrick Castle* included the town in its sailings in July and August as part of its programme, which took in various tours including Elie, Anstruther, May Island, St Andrews and the Forth Bridge, with one trip including an hour ashore to watch Kirkcaldy's Races and Games. The Galloway Saloon Steam Packet Company also ran regular trips in 1897 with *Stirling Castle* sailing from Leith to Kirkcaldy, giving visitors some time on land to look round the town.

CHAPTER 2

Extensions and Repairs

One of the earliest references to the harbour – probably on or near the present site – is in a charter of 1451 between the Abbot of Dunfermline and the burgesses of Kirkcaldy. An extract from the old Minutes in 1599 describes the decision of the Council for 'the biggin of a new pier' and a meeting was convened to decide exactly where it would be built, presumably at the mouth of the East Burn. But it's clear from the Minutes that the harbour was constantly at risk of damage from storms or from crumbling stonework; in 1663 it was reported that 'a breach in the new harbour has occurred. It is to be repaired with all diligence and all other apparent breaches there by wedging of the same with wedges as shall be thought most expedient, and ordinary stones lying in the quarry.'

A report in 1717 stated: 'Kirkcaldy harbour was wrecked through the last violent storm; some part of the pier met with such a disaster that it is broken through and through; it is recommended that the magistrates inspect the aforesaid disaster and employ workmen as they see fit.' By 1740 it was said to be in a ruinous condition. Although the west pier was built twelve years later, 'a storm in the spring did great damage to the pier and washed in great quantities of sand and sea water which filled the harbour as far up as the gangway'.

There was an ever growing number of complaints against Kirkcaldy Town Council for their failure to improve the structure of the harbour, which was said to be unsafe, incommodious and only accessible at spring tides to heavily laden ships. In 1756 the then Provost gave a report to the Council:

> The reason for calling this meeting is to inform you of the damage done by the late storm to the breakwater at the back of the harbour which had destroyed a great part of it. It is the general opinions of persons of skill that it is absolutely necessary to render the harbour safe, and that the addition of betwixt 30 to 40 feet should be made to the east head which would effectively protect the west. This would carry the easterly seas to the westward entirely free of the harbour. It will be necessary to repair it immediately to prevent more damage.

It was then unanimously voted by the Council 'to employ the magistrates to take any measures that they think proper for the immediate repair of the said breakwater, and to take the advice of an architect if they saw fit'.

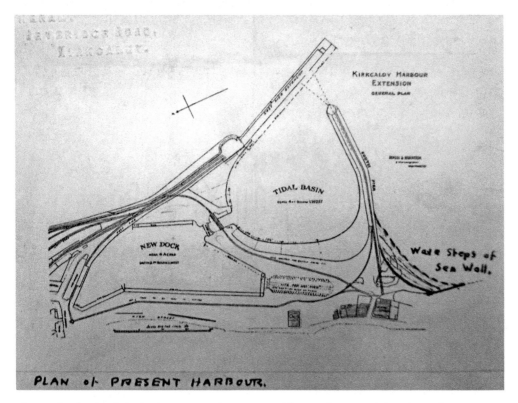

KIRKCALDY HARBOUR
EXTENSION
GENERAL PLAN

TIDAL BASIN

NEW DOCK

Water Steps of
Sea Wall.

PLAN of PRESENT HARBOUR.

This early sketch of the harbour gives the suggested layout for one of the planned extensions. (Kirkcaldy Galleries)

More damage was reported in January 1778 when Provost Dougall said: 'The great storm last week has beaten down a great part of the east head of the harbour, and all the breakwater and a number of stones were washed into the harbour mouth.' A succession of ideas for a new look to the harbour was put forward, such as the plan for improvements put forward by Edinburgh architect J. A. Craig in 1788, which came to nothing. In 1791 a subscription appeal was issued for contributions for funding for a new harbour. Almost fifty of the leading shipowners and public minded citizens of the day contributed to the subscription list, with wealthy shipowners such as Oliphant, Malcolm and Beveridge all putting in between two guineas and £5 to help swell the funds. Sir John Oswald of Dunnikier, the serving MP whose family owned the lucrative salt pans in the town, also offered ten guineas.

In 1804 the Provost reported: 'The west head of the harbour has come down and it is absolutely necessary to get it rebuilt; the cost of that plus repairing the east head has been estimated at upwards of £5,000 and considerably more will be needed.'

Although a new plan was submitted by Robert Stevenson in 1821, it took another twenty years before the latest plan by James Leslie of Dundee was adopted. In 1842 designs for a new extension pier were granted, when Provost Swan and the Harbour Commission decided to proceed with the expansion of a new wet dock and outer harbour. It was a great day for Kirkcaldy on 20 July 1843 when foundation stones were laid – all on the same day – for the new extension pier, a new Burgh School and an Episcopal Chapel. These

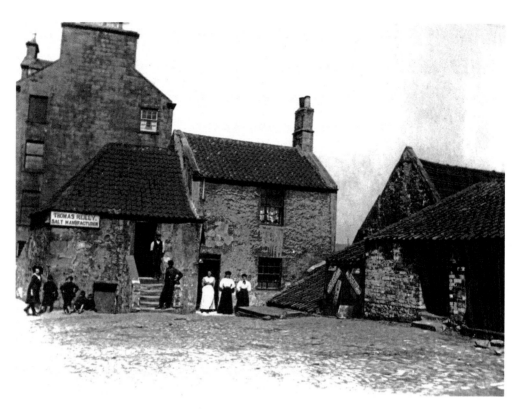

The Oswald family owned lucrative salt works.

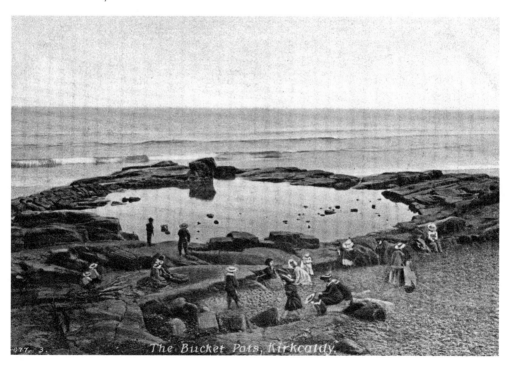

The Bucket Pats near the harbour collected salt water.

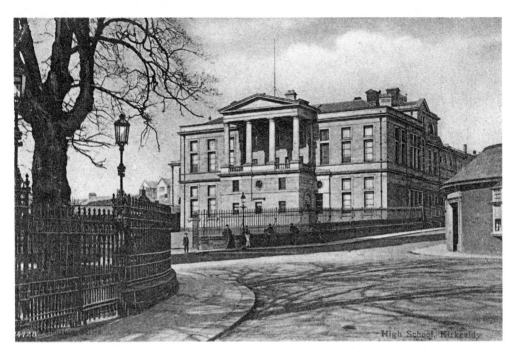

The foundation stone for the new Burgh School was laid in July 1843, one of three ceremonies performed on the same day.

activities were performed with great ceremony before, reportedly, some 7,000 and 8,000 excited citizens.

Andrew Beveridge recalled:

When I was very young I remember going down to see the laying of the foundation stone at the harbour extension. There was a Masonic procession with band and banners playing and great excitement, and the same day there was the laying of the foundation stone of the Episcopal Church in Townsend Place. The harbour extension was there before there was any thought of a railway being brought down. I remember dwelling houses to the east of the Harbour Head Hotel, and behind them I think there was a boat building yard.

In his speech at the opening ceremony, Provost Swan commented:

When the present work on the harbour is completed, I trust that it will be the means of opening up new channels for commerce and that it will add largely to the prosperity of the burgh. It is now almost 20 years since the last addition was made to the present pier and I trust that before the next 20 years have passed, a considerable addition will have been made to the west pier.

The Minutes also recorded that, in 1845, the Town Council resolved to improve matters by extending the east pier to the plan of Mr J. Leslie CE from Dundee at a cost of £10,000, but the completion of the plan would require £30,000 to £40,000. 'The Council wisely determined to proceed according to their means,' reported the Minutes, 'and not all at once

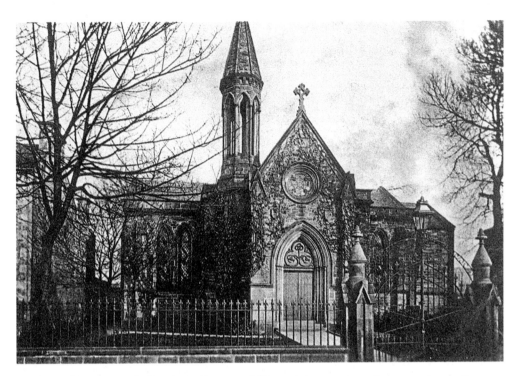

Work on the Episcopal Church in Townsend Place also started on the same day as the new harbour extension.

so as not to overburden the town with debt.' The new harbour, however, was opened the next year at the higher of the proposed costs. In the same year there was a proposal to have a train station at the harbour for not only goods but also for passengers:

> The Company will be obliged from the last day of March to the first day of October for a branch line to run four trains at suitable hours in each day, and three trains a day during the months of September to April, and four trains a day from March to October from the main line to the harbour of Kirkcaldy to convey goods and passengers, and shall return at the same number of times each day to suit the passing of trains both ways on the said main line.

The idea may well have been to give easy access to steamer day trips but no further reports have been found to show that a passenger train service was ever carried out.

During the succeeding years:

> The Harbour Commissioners did all that was possible to keep it in repair by blasting of rock, dredging the large banks of sand that accumulated in the fairway week by week, when tides and storms from the south-west played havoc with it. Steam ships were increasing in size and were sometimes obliged to land cargoes for our industries at Burntisland and at other harbours on the Forth and Tay.

Despite the harbour extension of 1843, with all its ceremony and brass bands, it was not seen in some quarters as an adequate improvement. Linen manufacturer J. T. Stocks,

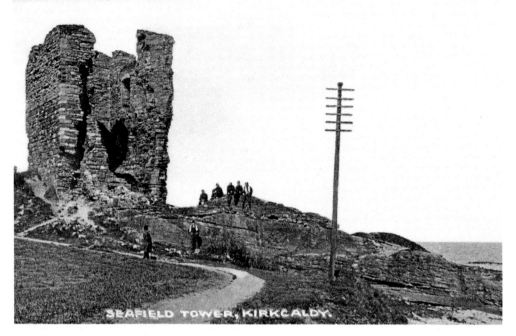

The ruins of Seafield Tower to the west of Kirkcaldy are all that remains of what was once an old feudal keep.

later Provost of Kirkcaldy, formed the London & Kirkcaldy Shipping Company in 1874 to improve the traffic at sea. He chartered vessels more suited to the bad conditions that prevailed at the old harbour entrance; he also decided to have his own ships built: the *Adam Smith*, the *Abden* (named after his farm in Kinghorn), the *Abbotshall* and lastly the *Kirkcaldy*. Over the years he kept urging the absolute necessity of a new and enlarged harbour to accommodate the increasing trade of the town, both in linoleum export and the paper trade.

In 1880 two new plans emerged: a proposed extension and rail connections direct to west Fife and Clackmannan, and a plan by William Kininmonth for a deep-water harbour and dock to cost £200,000. No records have been found that these suggestions were taken forward.

The next suggestion, however, was a serious proposal and a very contentious one: to build a new harbour and dock at Seafield, scarcely a mile to the west of the main harbour. In the 1880s and 1890s, a huge new harbour and dock complex was planned with a railway line and sidings, which would store up to 15,000 tons of coal for easy shipment, with a large warehouse to accommodate general cargo.

The *Fifeshire Advertiser* in June 1883 published a drawing showing the proposed Seafield plan:

> The dock will be situated on the coast between Tyrie bleach field and the ruins of Seafield Tower. The dock will be five acres in extent, and the work when completed will be protected by two breakwaters on the east and west Vous Rocks. The work when completed will effectually shelter the harbour from the prevalent storms from the east, which is the

direction from which storms of any magnitude would be likely to affect the dock. Once inside the breakwaters, comparatively smooth water would be reached. The entrance to the dock will be guarded by north and south piers so that vessels would easily pass into the outer basin and thence into the dock. The quay is proposed to be fitted with three coal hoists which would load 750,000 tons of coal per year so that adequate provision is made for the shipment of coal. The most important item in the enterprise is the depth of water on the dock sill, 30 ft at high tide and 13 ft at low water.

The *Cabinet Views of Kirkcaldy*, an undated book published probably in 1883 and illustrated with imaginative drawings of the future scene, also gave an enthusiastic description of the ambitious plans.

The Vous Rocks which at stream tides are only a few feet above high water, form an outer breakwater for the [proposed] harbour, and run parallel to and at a distance of about 250 yards from the sea wall. The entrance channel sheltered by these rocks will be about 300 yards long by about 70 yards wide, the width between the piers at the entrance to the tidal basin or harbour being about 80 yards. There will be a depth of 13 ft at low water and 30 ft at high water, of spring tides, and as the harbour and docks will be excavated to the same depth, ordinary coastal steamers will be able to enter at all times, while the largest class of vessels will be amply provided for at high water at any tide.

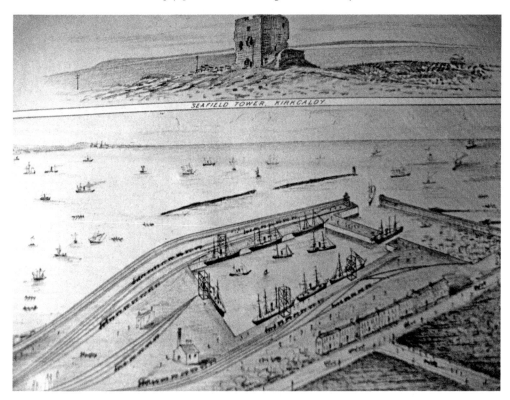

This sketch of the proposed new harbour and dock at Seafield featured in *Cabinet Views of Kirkcaldy*.

The outer harbour will cover about nine acres while the dock will occupy six acres in extent. Vessels calling with general cargoes and not requiring to enter the dock will have good quay space in the harbour, while fishing vessels will be accommodated on the beach where short jetties will be erected. Around the dock hoists are to be provided for the shipment of coal, with special cranes for general goods, all worked by hydraulic machinery. The space round the quay for railway sidings extends to about 16 acres, where from 12,000 to 15,000 tons of coal may be stored in trucks ready for shipment. It is anticipated that large warehouse accommodation will be required for general goods, and the ground adding the dock is well suited for these erections.

The completion of the enterprise is looked forward to with much hope by all classes of the inhabitants, as it will add greatly to the prosperity of the many important industries carried on in the district, develop more fully the mineral resources of the vicinity, and by attracting a larger population would increase the amenity, improve the buildings and conduce generally to the wellbeing of the people.

The book's accompanying artistic sketch showed the proposed harbour and dock with a dozen tall-masted ships in the harbour, countless ships in the Forth and a neat little railway track with coal trucks hauled by a steam train, all within a stone's throw of Seafield Tower. There was also the plan to run a railway along Sands Road (before the Promenade was built), running from Kirkcaldy dock to the proposed Seafield dock and harbour. Looking back now, it seems a puzzle as to why anyone would want to go to the huge expense of planning another harbour so near to the original one. From contemporary reports in the

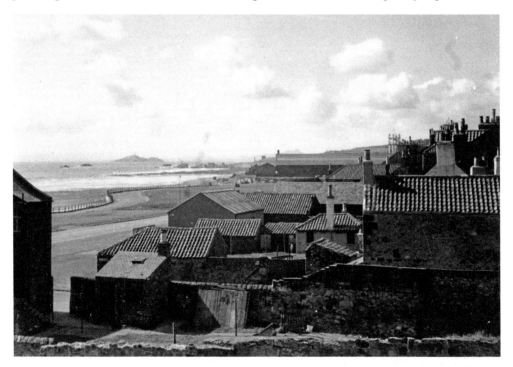

This overview from the Links area in about the 1930s shows the remains of the incomplete Seafield harbour in the distance.

local papers, however, it becomes apparent that the scheme's proposers were the owners of the Kirkcaldy & District Railway, who saw their chance of taking over the lucrative coal freight from the rival North British Railway Company. As the *Fifeshire Advertiser* again reported: 'This scheme has engrossed a good deal of attention lately, by the determined opposition which the North British Railway offered to the proposal.'

In a speech given to the Kirkcaldy Naturalists Society on 29 November 1890, Alexander Clark, who was the resident engineer of the Kirkcaldy & District Railway, explained the proposal.

After the failure of this proposed scheme in 1810, we are not aware that the project of constructing a harbour at Seafield ever disturbed the peace of anyone for more than 40 years, and only last year was the matter heard of again. It would be difficult to trace the reasons why this, with all its natural advantages, should have been so long neglected.

The reasons are these: 1. The harbour and dock will accommodate larger vessels than any of its rivals. 2. The entrance to the harbour is well protected and will make it less difficult to enter. 3. The railway connecting the docks and coal fields is shorter and more direct than the connection between the coal fields and any other docks.

Warming to his theme, Mr Clark added:

But the inhabitants have a great deal of work before them and they must be prepared for many sacrifices. Streets, lanes and closes must be widened, straightened and lightened so that its phenomenal darkness may be dispelled and all classes may know it as a place of comfort and safety. The town must assert its rights to possess a marine park and promenade and not thrust its slums into the forefront of its beautiful shore.

When the much longed for station connects the town to all parts of the country by means of two great railway companies bringing troupes of visitors to enjoy its marina, hotels and excellent sea bathing, the inhabitants will think in amazement through what stages can they have been allowed to pass.

A vision of utopia indeed.

The matter was seen as such an important and divisive issue that it was referred to a Select Committee of the House of Commons for a three-day debate. The many individuals and bodies who were strongly for the project included the provosts of Kirkcaldy, Dysart and Kinghorn, Kirkcaldy Harbour Commissioners, Stirlingshire and Fife County Councils and (needless to say) Kirkcaldy & District Railway Company – in all, more than 11, 000 signatures in favour. On the other side, those against the proposal included – again unsurprisingly – the North British Railway Company and the Earl of Mar, who owned the Great Northern & North East Railway Company.

The scheme went ahead; but although work was started on the new enterprise, it never reached anything like completion. The sum of £70,000 (a considerable sum in those days) was spent on starting to build the harbour, but presumably the cost turned out to be prohibitive and the consortium's money ran out. The scheme was then bought up by the rival North British Railway Company, which finished the railway line from Kirkcaldy to Auchtertool and Cowdenbeath for the use of mineral traffic only, but did not proceed with

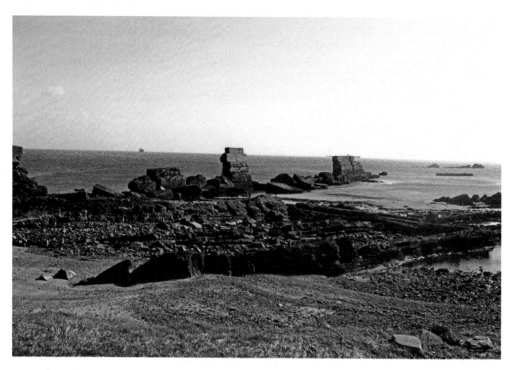

The sad remains of what was intended to be Seafield harbour are still visible from Kirkcaldy beach.

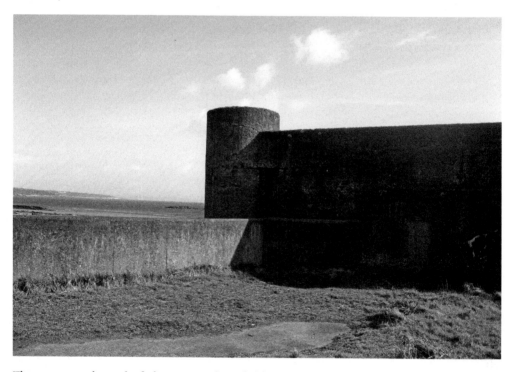

The turret at the end of the proposed Seafield harbour and part of the harbour wall still stand today.

the completion of the harbour itself. Part of the new sea wall gave way during a storm, leaving a gap in the concrete structure, and the project finally foundered. All that is visible now are a few concrete blocks and part of the harbour wall – sad reminders of what might have been.

Most surprising of all perhaps, in 1892 there was a move to drop any plans to improve the existing harbour: instead, there was a strongly suggested plan to build an additional new harbour at nearby Ravenscraig, near the grounds below Ravenscraig Castle. The Ravenscraig harbour plan had been proposed twenty years before by Sir John Coode, described as 'a very respected harbour engineer'. The plans at the time included a wet dock area of 8 acres, with 'quayage' of 2,100 feet and an added area of 10 acres with rail connections. There were to be four separate quays forming a square, with the south quay giving entrance to the harbour. This plan, although apparently given a great deal of thought and discussion, never came to fruition.

When a new harbour scheme costing £150,000 was considered in 1894, the *Fifeshire Advertiser* carried a stream of letters for weeks 'ranging from frank opposition through all phases of dubiety and conditional approval, to heavy support'. When plans were under way to upgrade the old Sands Road to what is now the Promenade, one letter stated: 'It may seem that as a community we should be seriously devising means for taking possession of the natural advantages which our fine run of beach affords.' There was also a proposal put forward in 1903 to include a new 'Promenade Pier'. It was suggested that this should

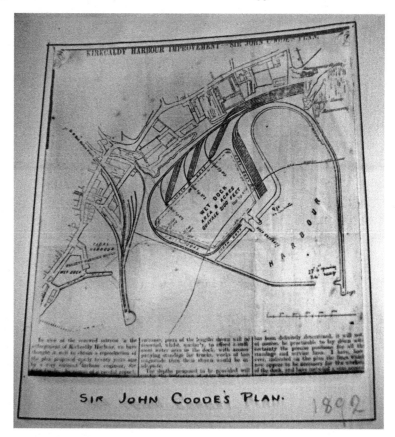

A completely new harbour at Ravenscraig was planned in 1892 by Sir John Goode but it never got off the drawing board. (Kirkcaldy Galleries)

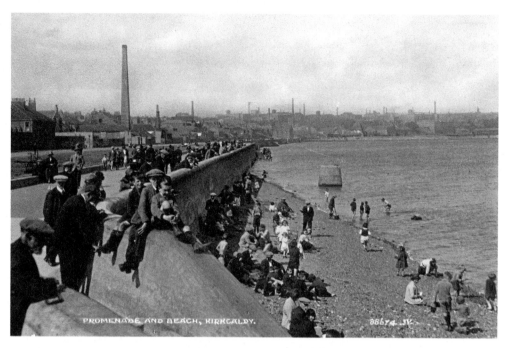

PROMENADE AND BEACH, KIRKCALDY. 88674 JV

Kirkcaldy Promenade was built in the 1920s, giving employment to local men who had come back from the trenches.

be built opposite the foot of Tolbooth Street, 'to be available for passenger steamers at all states of the tide, and would be an additional source of revenue'. Although the Prom was built in the 1920s, giving employment particularly to men who had come back from the First World War, the plans for the Promenade Pier were never carried out.

There were pages of letters in the *Fife Free Press* every week from 1900 onwards headed 'The Harbour Question'. One frustrated local man wrote:

Are we no nearer a deep water harbour than we were five years ago? If there was a harbour at Kirkcaldy and the necessary connection with the present system, a large amount of shunting might be provided between Seafield and the new links. The main difficulty is to connect the present railway line to the north of Kirkcaldy harbour taking account of the heavy gradient; but surely the railway enterprise is sufficient to overcome this obstacle even if it is necessary to tunnel from Ravenscraig to the lower level of the present line beyond Dysart?

The local paper's opinion column stated: 'Let us hope that ways and means will be found for providing what the town is very much in need of – a spacious deep water harbour equipped with the necessary railway for the delivery and loading of cargo.'

Another letter was published from the London & Kirkcaldy Shipping Company pointing out that their steamer *Abbotshall* was 185 feet long and there was just room to turn it around, and that their planned new steamer would be 15 feet longer; and that the harbour badly needed excavating, mainly to clear it from mud. A leading article in the paper in 1902 expressed the hope that ways and means would be found 'to provide what the town is very

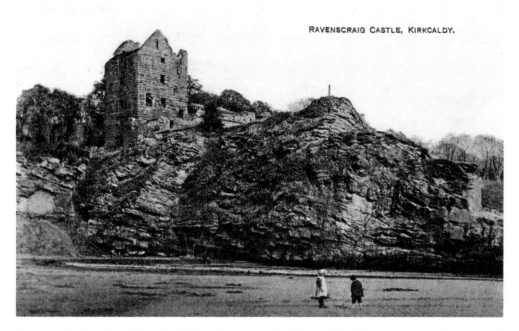

Ravenscraig Castle, built in the fifteenth century for Mary of Gueldres, was near the proposed site of Sir John Goode's harbour.

much in need of, a spacious deep water harbour equipped with the necessary railway for delivery and loading carriage'.

In October 1903 it was unanimously agreed that the Harbour Commission (which until then had been responsible for the harbour maintenance and operation) should be dissolved, and the harbour transferred back to Kirkcaldy Town Council and placed under its management.

Davidson's *Illustrated Guide to Kirkcaldy*, published around 1904, had some scathing words to say about Kirkcaldy's harbour as it was then:

In some respects our public men have strangely lagged behind in both the requirements of the town and in progressive public opinion. Our Harbour Commission is one of the glaring instances. In 1846 a sum of £40,000 was expended on an extension to the East Pier and other important improvements, but since then nothing of a permanent nature has been added to give increased facilities – if we except a breakwater built in 1859 which was laid in ruins by a storm within a few weeks. The efforts of the Commissioners have been directed by various methods – dredging, scouring etc towards the removal of accumulating mud, and blasting of rock inside the harbour itself, as well as at the fairway where large banks of drifted sand frequently accumulate in the course of a very few tides when storms blow from certain quarters.

This latter impediment has frequently detained our larger class of steam traders in the harbour for days, and prevented them gaining entrance until the 'trinket' was cleared away or the tides increased. With vessels, as with everything else, the trend of the times is to increase in size. To such an extent has this grown within recent years that nearly all

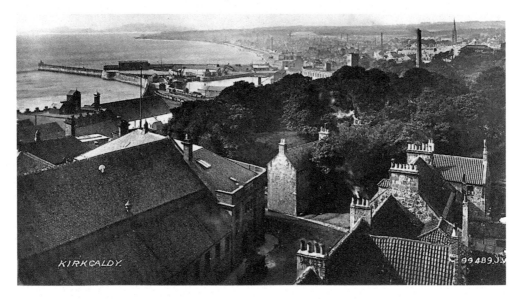

This view from the east shows the harbour with railway trucks and the building that operated the swing bridge.

the ocean going steamers are obliged now to land their cargoes of the raw materials for our industries at other harbours having proper dock accommodation and facilities in the Forth or Tay, and sent on by rail thereby considerably increasing the cost of transit.

Thanks to the enterprise of the late Provost Stocks years ago, and his worthy son today, we have three screw steamers: the *Abden*, with a carrying capacity of about 400 tons general cargo; *Abbotshall* with a general cargo capacity of about 450 tons, and the latest of the fleet, *Kirkcaldy*, which can carry about 540 tons on the London passage, each once a week. In October 1902 the Town Council unanimously resolved 'to take steps for the promotion of a scheme for a deep water harbour, and decided to appoint a strong committee after the November elections to carrying out the proposal'. This action was backed up a year later by the formation of a Harbour Extension Association, with a mass meeting of ratepayers held in the Adam Smith Hall.

Civil Engineer Sir A. M. Rendel of London was appointed to survey the foreshore and submit a report. His first plan with an estimate of £300,000 was decided to be too expensive, and he was asked to give an addition report with a modified scheme 'capable to being extended to complete the original scheme if this was advisable at some future date'. This second report was costed at around £107,000, which was to include an extension to the east pier, a new west pier, docks walls, gates and entrance machinery, and the excavation of the harbour and dock. This report was unanimously adopted by both the Town Council and the Harbour Commission, and the plan – along the lines which Provost Lockhart had campaigned for more than thirty years earlier – was eventually started in 1906. Local man William Mackenzie (eldest son of the last manager of Fife Pottery, which made the distinctive Wemyss Ware), who had just graduated in engineering from Edinburgh University, worked on the new extension as assistant to the Resident Engineer for Rendel & Robertson. He was directly responsible to Kirkcaldy Town Council as temporary Harbour Engineer, with

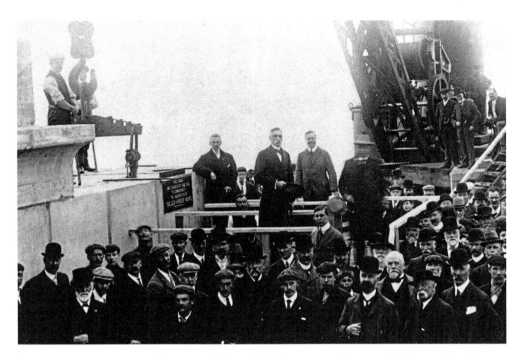

A stone to commemorate the start of the new harbour extension was laid in 1906 by Provost Barnet. (Kirkcaldy Galleries)

his responsibilities including supervision of contracts, preparation of specification and drawings for coal sidings, and general maintenance work – a vital and at times surely a daunting task for a newly qualified young man.

Provost Barnet laid a commemoration stone on 16 June 1906 to mark the inauguration of the New Harbour works, which were completed in 1909 and officially opened by the Earl of Elgin. Although Provost Stocks had died before the new harbour project began, his son Major Harris L. Stocks saw it come to fruition at last: indeed, the official opening was intended to be marked by the arrival of Stock's SS *Kirkcaldy*, but its thunder was stolen when a small sailing ship loaded with timber slipped into the new extension first.

CHAPTER 3

The Nineteenth-Century Whaling Industry

Kirkcaldy – along with many other ports in the UK – had a thriving whaling industry in the first half of the nineteenth century, with nine whaling ships registered in the port in 1828. The first Kirkcaldy whaler was *Earl Percy*, which set sail in 1813, followed over the years by *Triad, Rambler, Majestic, Chieftain, Caledonia, Viewforth, Ravenscraig, Regalia, Abram* and *Lord Gambier*. The town's last whaler, *Brilliant*, was bought from a Peterhead company, but after an unsuccessful voyage under Captain Hay, she was sold back to Peterhead in 1865.

Scotland as a whole became increasingly important as a whaling nation from the 1750s onwards. From 1750 to 1786, there were 367 whaling expeditions from Scottish ports, including ships from Kirkcaldy, Anstruther, Dundee and Aberdeen, at first to Greenland then later to the Davis Strait. The whalers usually left their home ports in March, often stopping off at Orkney and Shetland to recruit extra members of crew, and over the next two months worked their way northwards along the Greenland coastline to follow the whales as they were migrating.

As early as 1783, an advertisement appeared in the *Aberdeen Journal* looking for crews: 'Wanted for a ship to sail from Aberdeen next season, several stout lads as apprentices in the Greenland trade.' By the late eighteenth century, the average crew on a whaler was said to consist of the master, mate, surgeon, six harpooners, six steersmen, six line managers, six landsmen, six apprentices and seventeen sailors. There were also very specialised posts such as the spectioneer, who was the head harpooner and the most experienced on the ship. The word spectioneer is originally of Dutch origin, as indeed were many whaling terms, as the Dutch were the 'old masters' of whaling before the British took over in the eighteenth century, also taking some of their terminology. Very occasionally there was a post of Fishing and Ice Master: this was an indication that the whaler captain had little experience of sailing in the polar regions and needed an experienced man to guide him; this was rather like having a sailing master on some naval vessels who would perform the navigation for the captain.

Dundee was also an important whaling port, and the Dundee whaler *River Tay* was fitted out with steam engines in Kirkcaldy; being iron-built, however, the ice floes damaged her so much that she was withdrawn around 1865. Reports from the late 1880s show that several seamen with Kirkcaldy connections served on Dundee whaling ships, including

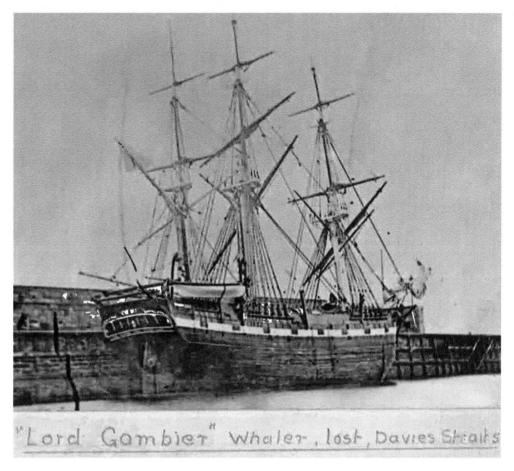

"Lord Gambier" Whaler, lost, Davies Straits

The three-masted *Lord Gambier*, built in Newcastle, was one of the Kirkcaldy whaling ships. (Kirkcaldy Galleries).

men such as John Beveridge, George Burnett (steward and harpooner), James McDougall, William Petrie and carpenter John Salmond. In some ports it was quite common for sons to follow their fathers into the whaling trade; their basic wage was not over generous, but this was augmented by bonuses as each of the men received a share of the catch. It was customary for the younger generation to start as 'green men' or inexperienced hands, working their way up to more specialised positions such as boat steerers, line handlers and then harpooners, with some eventually becoming a mate or master. Some of the men spent their entire adult lives whaling, while others made only one voyage and decided they had had enough: there were many potential dangers, including fog, storms and ice, American privateers and press gangs.

Details of their voyages and catches make uncomfortable reading now: in November 1833 the *Earl Percy* came back from the Davis Strait with 75 tons of blubber and whale bone, and in that one season, whaling ships brought home 900 tons of oil and 60 tons of whalebone with a total value of £30,000. In 1860 *Lord Gambier*, *Chieftain* and *Abram* accounted for a total of fourteen whales, with 200 tons of oil and 14 tons of whalebone. In 1868 *Ravenscraig* under Captain Allan brought back 4 tons of whalebone and 55 tons of

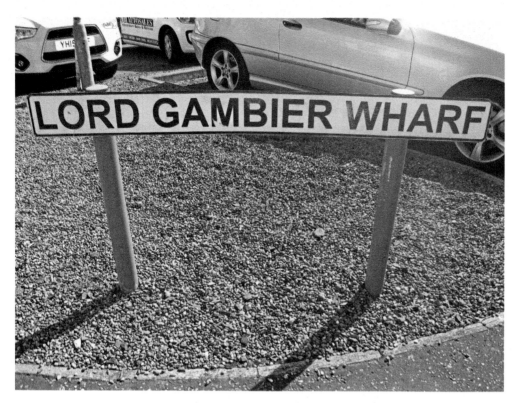

The street sign Lord Gambier Wharf on the recently built complex of housing on the harbour.

whale oil, and a year later the same ship arrived in Dundee with 4,000 seals and 42 tons of oil. Although it is a distressing period to read about, it remains an integral part of the life of the harbour along with the seafarers of the day and should be recorded. At the time it would no doubt be seen as a necessary industry and a way of making a living, as well as being a very hazardous one for the ships and crew with sub-zero temperatures, frostbite, lack of food and appalling conditions.

In 1835 it was estimated that eleven British ships were frozen up in the ice in the Davis Strait. One Kirkcaldy vessel, *Viewforth* (owned by Pratt of Kirkcaldy), under Captain Oliphant with officer William Elder – both members of prominent shipping families – was stuck fast in the Arctic ice with the crew suffering terribly from frostbite, scurvy and starvation as rations dwindled fast. Elder kept a meticulous and melancholy diary during the long months when *Viewforth* was trapped in the ice, and a contemporary writer, Revd J. Bain, published excerpts from his records, commenting that 1835 was one of the most eventful and disastrous years in the history of whale fishing.

The expedition report started off with some light-hearted moments, including an entry for 30 April that year. Elder reports: 'Exactly at noon "Neptune" went through his exercise of shaving, and no fewer than a dozen went through his hands. It is almost the only amusement sailors have got and they join in it with such glee. When at length up goes the garland on to the mast head, how proud we are that our ship looks as well as any of her consorts.'

By 20 May, *Viewforth* and her crew were among the Whale Fish Islands in Greenland and the atmosphere on board the ship was still buoyant. 'We have six Esquimaux aboard,' wrote Elder. 'They brought a fiddler along with them and in a start, all hands were out to get the 'tween decks cleared away, and there they lifted it [danced] in merry style for two whole hours. How happy the poor creatures were – I got a dart from them for some oaten biscuits; they went away as happy as if they had found a fortune.'

Elder also commented on the phenomenon of the halo of both the sun and the moon appearing at the same time in two or three luminous circles.

> The most brilliant and cheerful spectacle was the aurora borealis which tended to enliven the long gloomy nights. These fine works of nature are nowhere to be seen in perfection but in the distant north. We have also seen a beautiful comet-star over these past three nights; it bears NNW of us and has a very bright tail which all agreed to be exceedingly splendid and beautiful. Its tail had the soft appearance of the reflected light of an irradiated cloud.

This in fact would have been Halley's Comet, which had last been seen in 1759.

Other strange optical illusions and mirages were also noted:

> A never changing atmosphere, nowhere else to be seen than in those high latitudes, produces all sorts of shapes made by refraction on a scale of grotesque magnificence. The wild and futuristic forms which we behold cannot be described, and exceeded in variety the powers of the kaleidoscope itself.
>
> Midway in the air were mountains of icebergs of all sizes and shapes, and [what looked like] vessels suspended with their keels uppermost, sometimes with others beneath them with their top masts meeting each other.

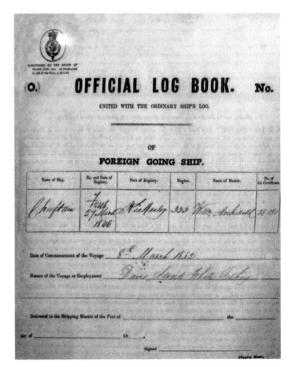

The whaler *Chieftain*'s log book lists their cargo of catches as well as a daily report on the crew's health and abilities. (Kirkcaldy Galleries)

But by 31 August, disaster struck and the ship and crew were locked in land ice in Brodie's Bay along with the *Jane* from Hull and the Aberdeen whaler *Middleton*. 'I have been ashore on the top of a high hill and saw nothing but ice,' wrote Elder. 'Now we are completely hemmed in and cannot move to any great distance.'

As time passed, rations started to run low: ship's biscuits, beef and meal were carefully measured out to the men but there was little fresh water left. To help eke out the dwindling rations, white foxes and ravens were caught as well as eggs from sea fowl. In common with the other whaling ships of the time, many of the men never survived to see their home ports again. While the ships in the same vicinity were able to communicate with each other, presumably by speaking trumpets, the feelings of isolation must have been intense.

By the end of October, morale was at a very low ebb, and fatalities increased, mostly from frostbite and from scurvy owing to the very limited diet for the men. Elder continued:

I can hardly write, my fingers are quite benumbed. Half our time is employed in working below deck and sometimes reading; I find it good to take exercises as it braces the nerves. We officers are more in the way of taking exercise which I think it the best antidote against scurvy, and I can almost say the only cure for it in the situation in which we are, now that the medicine is done. When any of the men now is needing physic, they are obliged to drink salt water.

Elder's diary entry for 4 December was deeply moving.

Another awful day such as I will never forget nor again behold. Another of our shipmates is gone, the poor fellow who was so bad last night. He slept away so quietly that no-one knew that the angel of death had passed over him until 7 am this morning. We sewed him

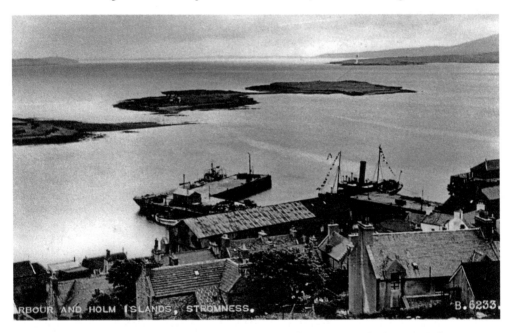

The whalers *Viewforth* and *Jane* finally sailed to safety in Stromness harbour in Orkney.

in a piece of canvas after making a hole in the ice and committed the body to the deep. We have been at death's door three or four times, but God has been merciful in delivering us so often from the jaws of destruction.

A deeply religious man, Elder held regular prayer meetings and readings, sometimes twice a day; in November he wrote in his diary, 'It was unanimously proposed by the men that we should all meet in the half deck, and give thanks to God who had so mercifully delivered us through the past week.' When they buried two more men at sea, Elder read sermons at the funeral services. He was quietly satisfied that 'the good effect of our meetings is making us all more agreeable, and laying aside swearing which I have not heard aboard this ship for many weeks'.

The crew were finally saved when the ship was eventually freed from the ice and drifted nearly 500 miles south until on 30 January they entered Stromness harbour, where the *Jane* had landed the night before. 'We were received by Captain Ross and the other officers and crew of the *Cove* with manifold demonstrations of joy and kindness.' But by the end of the whole disastrous voyage, *Viewforth*, which had been eleven months at sea, had lost six of her crew, and *Middleton* had lost eight.

The official report of the voyage stated:

There is ample evidence that the attentions of Captain Oliphant and the surgeon were unremitting, and that they availed themselves of all the limited resources within their reach. Our wonder is that the mortality was not greater, and when we consider the dangers to which so many others became sacrifices but out of which this ship was brought, we cannot withhold our admiration of the skill and perseverance by which it was accomplished.

As in other classes of ships and sailors, there were many superstitions adhered to among the whaling fraternity. In Whitby for instance, the wives of the whalers contributed to the success of the voyages by throwing shoes to wish their men good luck, and wearing their 'shifts' inside out in a bid for good weather and a successful trip. But it was also considered to be bad luck to have a woman on board a whaler (or indeed on some fishing boats). One captain made sure he always carried a 'lucky penny' on board his ship. There was a widespread belief that Friday was an unlucky day to start a voyage, although different parts of Scotland had varying 'lucky days'; whalers and fishermen from the East Lothian area thought that Sunday was the best day for sailing, but few if any other ports shared this belief. Some animals and birds were thought to be weather omens – the sighting of porpoises or dolphins was favourable, unless they jumped clear of the water as this was thought to herald a storm.

Another insight into the conditions for the whaling ships and their crews came in Thomas Williamson's memoir written in 1873:

My Uncle Robert Oliphant was a clever, active young man who got command of one of his uncle's vessels before he was 20. After sailing for several years in different vessels, he retired and conducted his business. Latterly he took charge of the Kirkcaldy company, the Greenland Whale Shipping Company, a very large and lucrative business. His partners

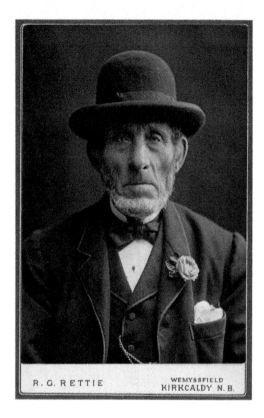

R.G. RETTIE WEMYSSFIELD KIRKCALDY N.B.

Captain Robert Ritchie was skipper of the *Triad*, the first vessel to arrive home from Russian ports since the Crimean War. (Kirkcaldy Galleries)

were Mr Pratt (owner of *Viewforth*), Mr Dougall and others. It was on the whole a prosperous career but it was a cold dangerous business, and woe to the crews of any ship that got beset on the ice and was kept all winter in Greenland.

William Oliphant was a shipmaster and shortly before his death commanded one of the Greenland whale ships. His vessel was unfortunately beset with the ice about September just before they were leaving for home, and was kept fast among the thick ribbed ice. They had to endure the misery of a cold and totally dark winter except what light came from the moon and stars. I remember the sad state we were all in when it was known they were beset in the ice; no help could be sent until spring when the vessels would again be going out.

He also recalled other family members:

When Uncle Robert died, my cousin Henry managed the business. He had several ships, *Brothers, Favourite, Firm,* and *Friends.* They went principally to Holland, Heligoland, the Baltic and the Mediterranean, and he used to command one of them. On one trip to Rotterdam when he was a young man he fell in love with a young Countess, or she with him, but his friends stopped the romance. She gave him some fine diamond shoe buckles which afterwards he gave to my mother and they were in our family for a long time. One was made into a beautiful crescent shaped brooch and presented to my daughter Anne Mary on her marriage to Charles Macdonald of the East Indies – a nice heirloom, and valuable too.

The crew might number about 60 or more and the provisions would fall. After a horrid winter, a heavy gale whirled down the whole sea of ice, ship and all, and often she was twisted like a cork on the water until she got out into open water and the poor remnant of the crew managed to get sail on her. They got to the Orkneys and got relief, and with a fresh crew at last got to the Firth of Forth and home, but few survived. Starvation, cold and broken spirits did their work among a great many, and their bodies lay unburied in the snow.

When William Oliphant came home his spirits were crushed and his constitution broken, and he gave up thoughts of going to sea again. He told me: 'When I saw the ship was fairly and firmly fixed after all our efforts to saw her out of the ice, and all the other ships away, I nearly gave up in despair. I called the officers and crew and said that we must do our best to live until relief came in the spring; that we must go on short allowance and try, by burning the blubber and what wood we had or could gather, to endeavour to have light and fire to cook with; that I would share all I had with them and do all I could to comfort them. By and by the sun disappeared and then nothing but gloom, we were far off land and the white Greenland bears were our companions. The cold got intense, far below zero, even freezing the rum and brandy. Some of the men got sulky and obstreperous, some cried, some got ill, some began to die and we just had to lift them out of their hammocks and lay them on the ice alongside the ship, covered with a little snow. Before we got clear in January there were thirty bodies buried in the same way all lying around us, in fact at the end we had scarcely strength left to remove them out of the ship.

Accustomed as I was at home to every comfort, the contrast now was dreadful but hope kept burning beside my glimmering lamp. How we used to dish out and divide our scanty store! our hard biscuits were worth gold to us, we brought some home with us and our friends would ask one as a relic.

When he finally got home to Kirkcaldy, William stayed at home, content to watch the ships leave port again in the spring. However tragedy overtook him – ironically enough for someone who had survived the dangers of an Arctic winter – in the waters of the Forth. He boarded a small pleasure boat accompanied by a friend to sail to nearby Dysart; but shortly after leaving Dysart harbour and not far from shore, a sudden breeze caught the

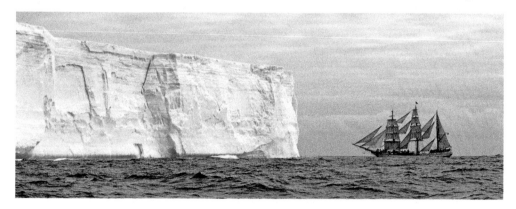

This modern photograph shows the scale of a huge iceberg east of South Georgia with the three-masted barque *Europa*, which was launched in 1911. (Phil Wickens)

sail and upset the boat, which suddenly sank, taking William with it. Although boats went out and dragged the Forth in all directions, his body was not found for several weeks until it was washed up on Kirkcaldy sands.

A copy of *Chieftain*'s log book dated March 1841 from the Davis Strait, written up in beautiful copperplate by master Robert Tod, lists their cargo of seventy casks of blubber, whale bones and jaw bones: uncomfortable reading today, but again of its time. Reports from the same ship in 1852 under Captain William Archibald include a daily report on the crew, with marks for ability in seamanship, their conduct on board, and details of treating illnesses such as glandular fever and gastritis.

In 1847, *Chieftain* arrived home bringing news of the loss of the *Caledonia* in the ice. The *Abram* sailed from Kirkcaldy, hiring extra crew in Shetland to hunt whales in the Arctic in 1862; the wooden vessel was caught in a storm and was crushed between two huge sheets of ice. The crew had just time to scramble off the ship on to the ice floes and were later rescued. The *Lord Gambier* was lost in 1862 but several of the crew were saved and looked after by the native Inuits until they were able to return home. Crews from *Abram* and *Chieftain* were also helped to survive by the Inuits.

An official report of the conditions for British whalers in the 1830s included the damning paragraph that 'the whalers were ill prepared both in provisions and equipment, and in techniques of hunting and travel to survive an Arctic winter. Shipowners' assumption that provisions supplied were enough was dangerously unsound.'

Andrew Beveridge recalled:

When we were young we got a day's holiday from school to see the whaling ships sail for Greenland. My own father went to sea; he went for two seasons to the Greenland whale

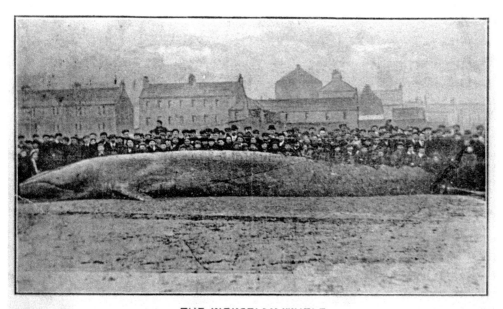

M. & L. PAGE.   THE KIRKCALDY WHALE.   Photo. by A. G. Adamson,

A whale was washed up on Kirkcaldy beach in 1904, much to the interest of the townsfolk. (Kirkcaldy Civic Society)

fishing and after that to a King's Revenue cutter probably sent out to watch for smugglers. When he returned home he became skipper of the first steamboat to ply from Anstruther and Kirkcaldy to Leith, then he became manager of the Kirkcaldy and Leith boats where he remained for many years. Near the harbour there was a boiling house for the oil brought in by the whaling ships so that it could be processed there.

The oil boiling house was looked at enviously by Kirkcaldy's neighbouring burgh of Dysart, 3 miles to the east. Dysart Town Council wanted a part of the lucrative business and decided to build its own oil shed beside the inner harbour there. Although completed in 1835, it was never used, as the local landowner, the Earl of Rosslyn, was horrified at the thought of the smell of whale oil polluting his estate, part of which bordered on to the harbour. He applied for an interim interdict to stop the building going up, and when the town carried on regardless he took his appeal to the House of Lords. He won his case and the oil shed, although completed, was never used for its original purpose.

Beveridge wrote:

It used to be a grand sight for us boys to see the Greenland ships going away in spring and coming home about July and August with full ships. The pieces of whale and live bears caused us great fun and once they brought a young Esquimau. The vessels lay in the bay and we used to pull off in our boats to see them. The ships had flags and a garland at the mast head; if however any of the ships had lost an officer or man during the voyage, when coming up the Firth their flags were only half mast high; then it was a sad scene.

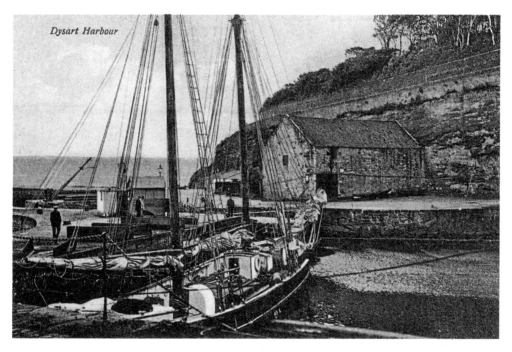

The oil shed at Dysart harbour was built in 1835 to take advantage of the lucrative whaling business, but was never used.

The 'young Esquimau' remembered by Beveridge was a thirteen-year-old Inuit boy called Akkatook, known in Kirkcaldy as Kookie Ekie. His home was somewhere near Baffin Island, and he had been so fascinated by seeing the whaling ships from Scotland that he asked if he could go back on one of the ships to see this foreign land for himself. The idea was backed by his parents, and he was given into the temporary care of Captain Kinnear of the Kirkcaldy whaler *Caledonia*. Needless to say, his arrival in Kirkcaldy was greeted with amazement and wonder, and he was given a warm welcome.

The *Fife Herald* of 3 December 1846 published the following account in the flowery and often rather patronising language of the time:

> The young stranger Kookie Ekie, brought here some weeks ago by one of the whale ships of this port, has since his sojourn in this town not only become an object of attraction to the community, but has been taken under the special patronage of the gentry who have bestowed on him every kindness and attention.
>
> They have metamorphosed his condition of life from that of a rude denizen of nature's frigid wilderness, to a smart looking sprig of gentility, having dressed him in a new suit of fashionable clothes. His savage dress of sealskin he only resumes when invited to visit any of the baronial seats in the neighbourhood such as Raith, Dysart, Balbirnie, Wemyss Castle. There he has shown with what dexterity he can use the bow and spear and manage his canoe, which implements he always takes with him on such occasions.

He was described in the newspaper article as 'a lad of about 14 years of age, stout made, broad features, dark sharp eyes, jet black glossy hair with a little tinge of sallow in his complexion, and seems quite at home. As he is apt to learn, it is to be hoped that the

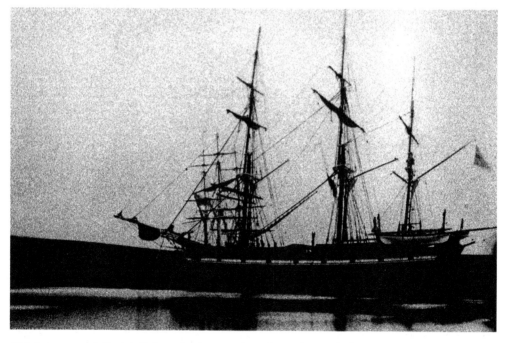

Chieftain rescued Kookie Ekie and crew members from the ice floes. (Kirkcaldy Galleries)

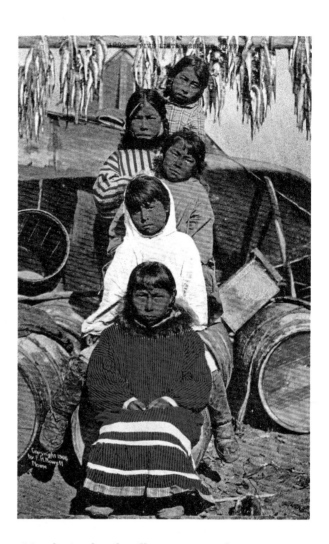

This old photograph shows Inuit girls around the same time as young Akkatook came to Kirkcaldy.

experienced teacher under whose tuition he is placed, will use every endeavour to pour instruction into his untutored mind.' He stayed with Captain and Mrs Kinnear until the spring when the whalers started out again for the long and perilous journey back to the Davis Strait. Before he left, he took part in the local regatta to demonstrate his skills with his canoe or kayak, both in the harbour and along the shore, where 'troops of the curious lined the shore for upwards of a mile. The exhibition was made on Saturday in the presence of a considerable concourse of people of all classes.'

He was given a selection of gifts to take home, including 'several suits of clothes, cloth, blankets, pots and pans, firearms etc, and a mind stored with the many wonderful sights which he has seen while here. He will bear with him the good wishes of all who know him.'

The journey home in the same ship with Captain Kinnear was fraught with danger: like so many whalers, *Caledonia* was crushed in the ice and wrecked. Most of the crew including Kookie Ekie just managed to escape, although many of his presents were lost. The crew were rescued by *Chieftain*, another Kirkcaldy whaler, and the young Inuit was taken home safely; meanwhile, all those who had met him in Kirkcaldy would no doubt talk about him and the whole experience of his culture for the rest of their lives.

CHAPTER 4

Shipowners and their Houses

A trades directory of 1825 lists the names of forty-one shipowners in Kirkcaldy at that time, an indication of just how important the harbour was, and how very wealthy these families became carrying out their import and export trade. Two of the most important families were the Malcolms, who had six ships, and the Oliphant family, who owned five. Other well-to-do mariners, merchants and ship-owning families included Balfour, Beveridge, Bogie, Dougal, Elder, Fergus, Jamieson, Law, Mackie, Millar, Stocks, Swan and Williamson, with their vessels including both cargo ships and whalers.

It was logical therefore that local shipbuilding yards did a flourishing trade to supply the demand for large ships. Engineers James Brown had two shipyards; one was to the west of the Tiel Burn and built *Windover*, *Sunbeam* and *Tiel* for the Kirkcaldy, Leith & Glasgow Shipping Company, which was set up in 1808 to give local traders a daily service to Leith, as well as a weekly service to Glasgow via the Forth & Clyde Canal. Brown's other yard was close to their engineering works on Sands Road (which much later became Kirkcaldy Promenade), near Rose Street, supplying two iron brigs, *George Ann* and *Eliza*, for the Swan Brothers. KL&G had another two ships built, SS *William Yule* and SS *John Strachan*, both named after two local directors. By the nineteenth century Kirkcaldy depended heavily on the shipping and whaling industries for its prosperity, with the revenue from the harbour being the town's principal income.

It can come as no surprise that many of the wealthy shipowners and merchants chose to build or to live in their grand houses as close to the harbour as possible. Most of these houses have sadly disappeared over the passage of time, but fortunately at least three have not only survived the centuries, but have been sensitively renovated and restored. Prominent shipping families, including the Oliphants, Laws, and Malcolms, lived in substantial and often very grand houses opposite the harbour. Some of these have still survived: Law's Close or the Merchant's House, Harbour House near Fish Wynd, and Sailors Walk are all very fine buildings, and have been restored and preserved in recent years.

An early Ordnance Survey map of 1824 shows not only the houses but the names of the people who lived there, with the name Oliphant – possibly the most powerful and wealthy family of all the Kirkcaldy shipowners and sea captains – shown at least five times on

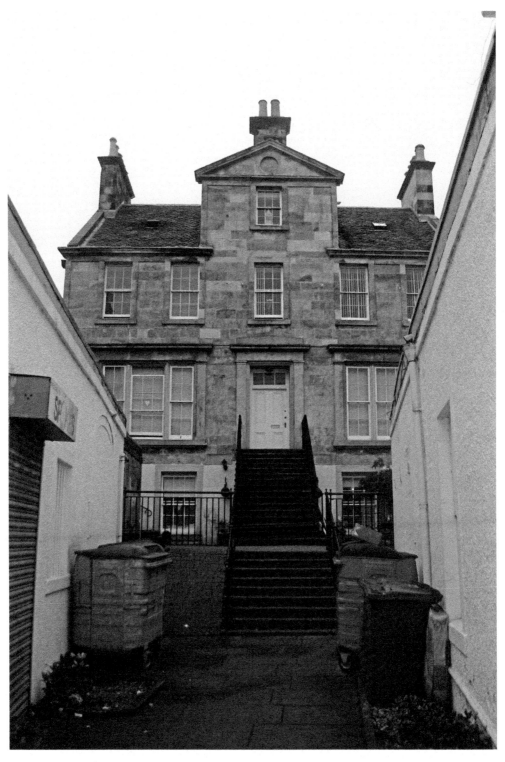

Harbour House at Kirkcaldy's east end may well have belonged to one of the Oliphant shipowners.

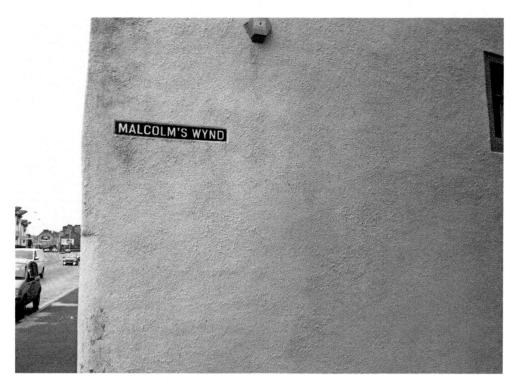

The name on this narrow lane commemorates the wealthy ship-owning Malcolm family.

different properties. The Malcolm family had three properties as well as having one of the narrow wynds named after them, with the street sign still extant.

What is thought to be Kirkcaldy's oldest house at 443–449 High Street, built around the fifteenth century and originally known merely as the Auld Hoose, was originally a block of up to five separate residences along with the Customs House.

Over the years, the Auld Hoose became so badly run down that it came within a whisker of complete demolition between the two world wars. A slim booklet entitled *Kirkcaldy's Oldest House: A Plea for its Preservation*, by G. M. Lendrum – undated but written in the early 1930s – put forward a well thought out and passionate plea for the building to be rescued.

'After the demolition [in 1931] of Kirkcaldy's Gladney House, birthplace of architect Robert Adam, surely there is no need for the ruthless destruction of more historic old buildings?' wrote Mr Lendrum in his introduction. He continued:

> Now we are left with one ancient residence which it is to be hoped will be saved for posterity. This is the old house on the Sailors' Walk, claimed by some to be as old as Ravenscraig Castle which was built in 1459. Be this as it may, it has overlooked the ever changing stream of life which has passed beneath its venerable walls for nearly four centuries. Of Flemish design, its crow-stepped gables and graceful corbellings have attracted the interest of more than one artist visiting the town. Its story has so far remained elusive and obscure, though it is believed that it was originally built for a wealthy trader in the days when Kirkcaldy was a seaport of consequence.

The old folk of the town tell many tales of the Royalties who had dined and even lodged therein. There is no reason to dispute this, for evidences of past glories are still to be found in some of the rooms, one of which is decorated with roses, thistles and fleur-de-lys in stucco. This particular room is sometimes alluded to as 'The Queen Mary Room' – many legends abound regarding her supposed stay here and it is quite likely that she may have broken some of her many journeys through Fife at this resting house. It is even more likely that Mary of Guise stopped within its ancient walls, for it is stated on good authority that she passed through Kirkcaldy with her French soldiers. Prior to this, King James is reported to have sailed from our harbour when he went to France to fetch his Queen. This urges one to think that he also may have called at the old house before embarking.

According to a local worthy, there is a subterranean passage which once connected the inn with a certain hole in the harbour wall, down which many a cask of good Rhenish wine and other contraband was smuggled into the town from ships trading with foreign parts.

The eastern side of the building which faces Malcolm's Wynd has a large Coat of Arms of Charles II bearing the date of 1662 or 1682; if the date is 1662 that is the year that His Majesty confirmed the Royal Charter of the town. It is asserted that he stopped at the old house when he passed through Kirkcaldy in 1650 after his coronation at Scone.

Lendrum also provided a carefully detailed chart naming the original occupants of what were once five separate dwellings within the building, with some names going back as far as 1650. Although the owners (or tenants) originally included names such as Patrick Jackson, James Pittilloch (mariner), David Laing, Robert Brown (mariner) and Patrick Rankin, by the mid-1800s all the houses had been bought or inherited by the wealthy and powerful William Oliphant. Henry Oliphant, for instance, who was grandson of one of the original owners, sold his house to his uncle for £1 10s in the late 1700s. No wonder, then, that for many years afterwards it was referred to locally as Oliphant's House, and it must have been an ideal vantage point from where a shipowner could keep a close eye on his vessels coming into and leaving the harbour opposite.

There seemed to have been a great deal of intermarriage among the owners or occupants of the various flats of the old house and their near neighbours, with Oliphants marrying Barkers or Browns and Williamsons marrying Oliphants. William Oliphant took the trouble to nominate several people – all noted and worthy residents of the town – to act as trustees of his property after his death. Robert Nairn of floorcloth manufacturing fame, Patrick Don Swan, manufacturer and later Provost of Kirkcaldy, Samuel Davidson of the Commercial Bank and manufacturers William Beveridge and John Kay were all appointed as trustees. By 1888 all but two of these men had themselves died and the house was sold to George Landale, who (at the time of Lendrum's record) had left it to his sons, who had settled in British Columbia.

Lendrum ended his book on a sentimental note:

Memories come crowding into mind, but the old house still stands as a silent witness of days which are gone. Is it to receive the same fate as Gladney House? Are we in Kirkcaldy, and our friends at home and abroad, going to stand by while anther demolition takes place? It is to be sincerely hoped that we can save this ancient though dilapidated relic of an historic past for the generations to come.

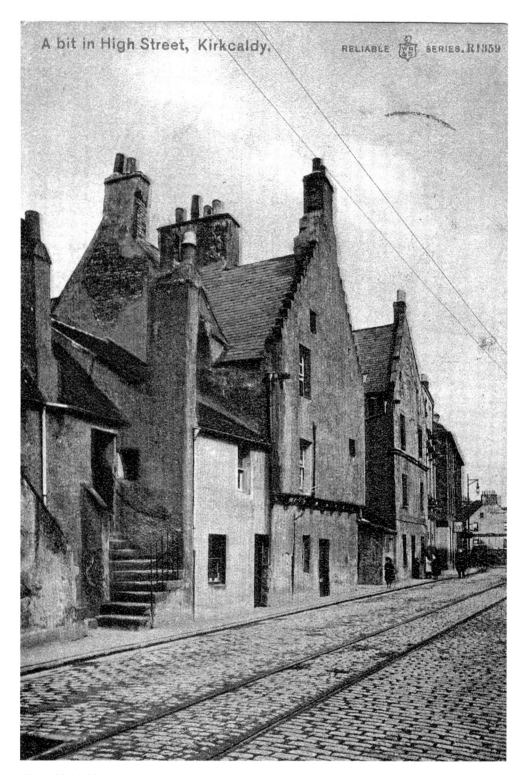

This old building was originally known as the Auld Hoose and housed several families, including the Oliphants and their relatives.

His well-researched book must have been one of the important factors to bring the plight of the old house to the attention of the local public, and in the early 1930s a far-seeing local committee launched a public appeal to save it. It was taken over by the National Trust for Scotland in 1935 and after the war years it was finally restored to its former glory with additional funding from the Historic Buildings Council and from local individuals. As the house had been built on a stretch of the High Street near the harbour called Sailors Walk, it took this name after its renovation. And it was certainly well worth restoration: among its interior features there are wooden beams inscribed with Biblical texts, a sixteenth-century ceiling decorated with fish and flowers, fleur-de-lis and thistles on the walls in plaster, a bed which slid into a stone recess and a stone mantelpiece with the date 1667 and the initials R. and B.W.

An old recorded memoir by George Oliphant recalled:

The Auld Hoose, that big old house, still to be seen standing at the top of the west quay and overlooking the Firth of Forth, looks like a strong oak of the forest. It has withstood many a gale and has witnessed many a change. All who used to live and sport in it are gone: how many associations does it bring forth, how many ghost stories were told in it?

A later Ordnance Survey map of 1951 shows a row of houses named Oliphant's Terrace between Malcolm's Wynd and Fish Wynd, and surprisingly there is still a street sign remaining on the nearby wall saying 'To Oliphant's Terrace'; the remains of demolished

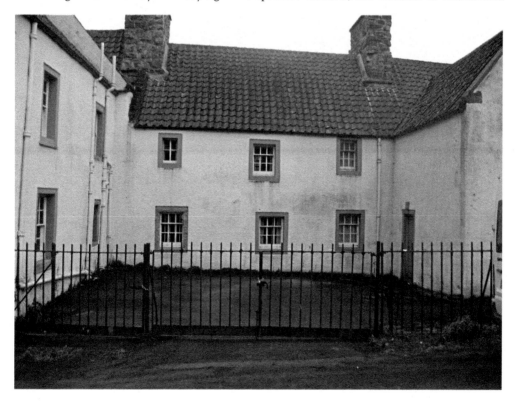

The rear view of Sailors Walk.

buildings and two old fireplaces may have been part of the original terrace. Near this site may also have been the original 'kailyard', which William Oliphant acquired in the early eighteenth century and turned into a garden.

George Oliphant, shipowner and sea captain, also lived in Kirkcaldy, although his voyages took him far afield. Thomas Williamson, who was born in 1804, had the foresight to collect a unique record of family memories with first-hand recollections of the late eighteenth and early nineteenth centuries:

> My Uncle George was one of those who lived in stirring times, with wars and rumours of wars. In his younger days, America had thrown off her allegiance to England so we had America and her privateers against us, and Emperor Paul of Russia was ready at any moment to declare war against England. Later on was the horrid war with the French and Danes, when Nelson like a defiant messenger of wrath bore down upon Denmark and at Elsinore scattered her noble fleet, and at the Nile and Trafalgar he destroyed and segregated the fleets of France and Spain. My Uncle George lived in all these eventful times down to the close of the continental war in 1815 at Waterloo. It was very amusing to hear the conversations that went on with my uncle and some of the old sea captains. They talked about freights, convoys, charters, ships being taken as prizes, Llloyd's List, how much they cleared on the last voyage, how the Custom House officers behaved, and so on.

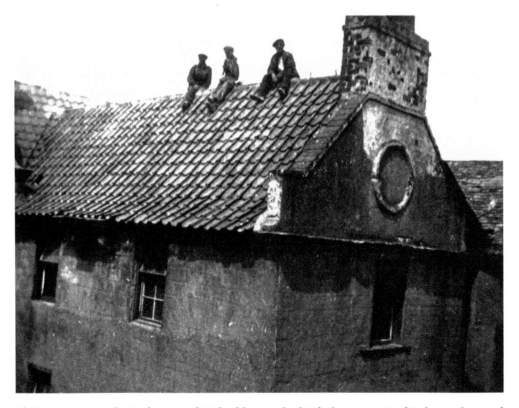

Gladney House in the Links area of Kirkcaldy was the birthplace in 1728 of Robert Adam and was demolished in 1931.

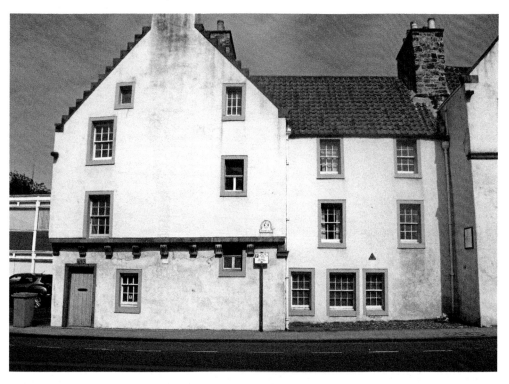

The Auld Hoose was taken over by the National Trust for Scotland in 1935 and was later restored to its former glory and renamed Sailors Walk.

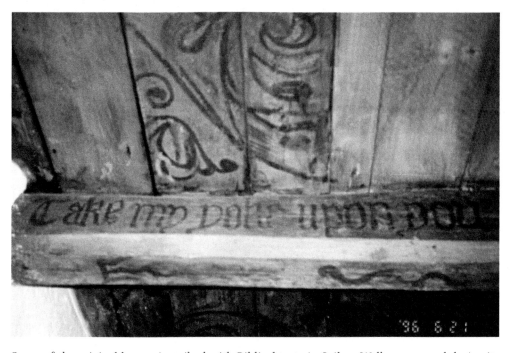

Some of the original beams inscribed with Biblical texts in Sailors Walk were saved during its renovation. (Kirkcaldy Civic Society)

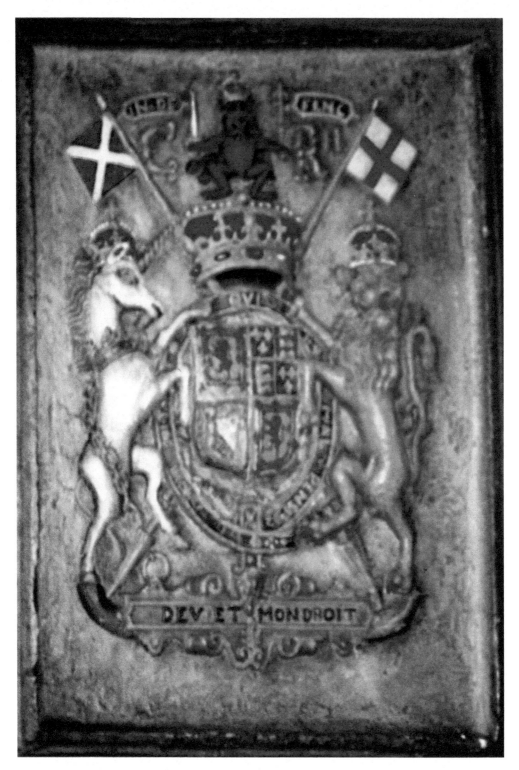

This fine coat of arms with the motto 'Dieu et mon Droit' has also been preserved in one of the rooms in Sailors Walk. (Kirkcaldy Civic Society)

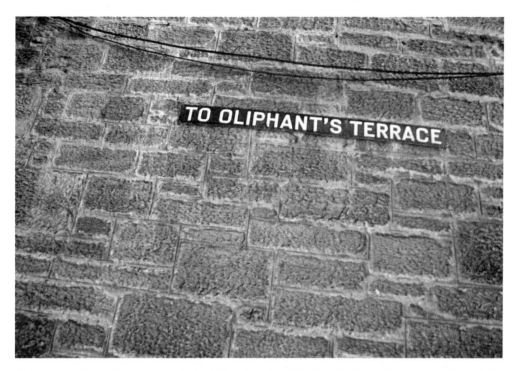

This street sign still remains of the side of wall of Sailors Walk, a direct reminder of the Oliphant family.

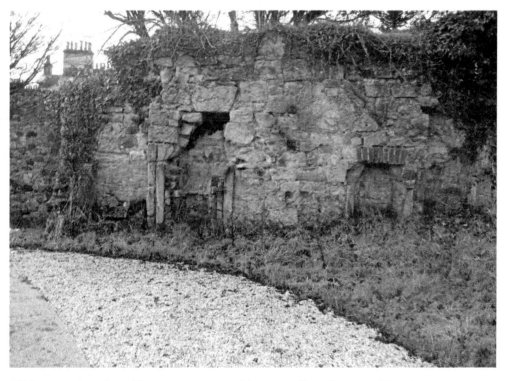

All that remains of an old terrace are some old stone walls and traces of fireplaces.

The memoir gave another eye witness account of Paul Jones' ships in the Forth.

When George was a boy of about 12, he and his older brother Robert took a sail out to their uncle's vessel to spend the day on board in the Firth of Forth, when they saw three ugly vessels beating up the Firth and standing close to where they were. They had American flags at their mastheads and they soon found out they were the ships of the famous John Paul Jones. His ships tried to beat up to Leith to land and plunder the town but the wind blew too hard and they abandoned the attempt and sailed down the Firth again. The boys got safely ashore helped by my mother, as all on shore were in great distress as they feared Paul Jones might board their vessels and carry off the crew – he was a great vagabond, Paul Jones. He eluded our men-of-war and was never caught.

Thomas Williamson's memoir recalled another adventure by George Williamson:

One voyage Uncle George took was when we were at war with the Danes: his vessel was one of the Baltic Fleet which had all congregated at Leith Roads in a convoy – the only safe way they could go abroad and always with one or two ships of war to accompany them on the voyage. The West India convoy met at the Cove of Cork, one at Greenock and one at the Downs. The ships had to keep as close together day and night with signals in case any stray vessels fell behind. Passing near one of the Danish forts, the Danes began to fire and one ball went through the main top sail which angered my uncle: he put his speaking trumpet to his mouth and roared out: 'Avast firing there, you cowardly rascals, do you mean to hurt people?' Then turning to the man at the helm, he said 'Don't be frightened, Davie, keep her full and don't mind those cowardly beggars; if I had them in Kirkcaldy they would pay sweetly for that top sail.' I believe they all got safely up the Baltic.

Another voyage he took was to Russia; we were at peace with Russia when he left Kirkcaldy but Paul was Emperor or Tsar, and England at the time never could tell what a day would bring forth. Paul used to annoy the English captains by the absurd orders he issued: one day an Imperial Order would come out that 'all the English must appear in cocked hats'; another 'all the English must appear in knee breeches'; and another that under the threat of being exiled to Siberia, all the English must appear in plain hats.

My uncle – not dreaming that war would be declared so suddenly by Russia against England and having heard nothing of it when he left – sailed up quite pleasantly and anchored at Cronstadt. The Custom House officers came on board as usual and shook hands; shortly after that some Russian officers came on board, fine fellows with feathers in their hats. I must tell it in Uncle George's words: "Good morning gentlemen, hope you're well, how's my good friend the Emperor? Glad to see you, what will you take? I have some fine London porter on board, or Edinburgh strong ale and Scotch whisky, anything you like, gentlemen." Then the officers said: "Oh thank you very much, Captain Oliphant, you're very kind, but we have bad news for you: the Emperor has declared war a few days ago against England, and you will have to give us your ship's papers as we must lay an embargo on your ship. You will require to go with us as prisoners of war and march up to the interior."

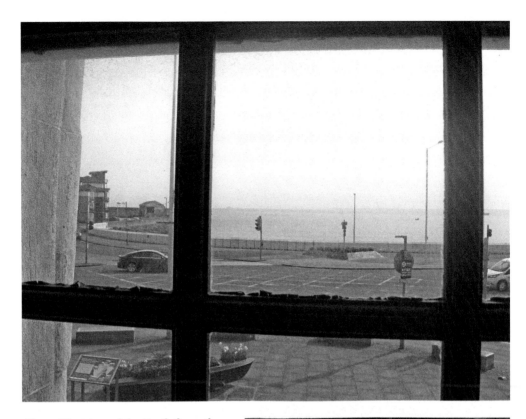

Above: The view of the Forth from the window of Law's Close.

Right: Tsar Paul I was Emperor of Russia from 1796 to 1801, when he was assassinated by a group of civil and military officials.

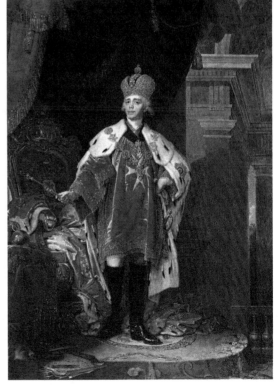

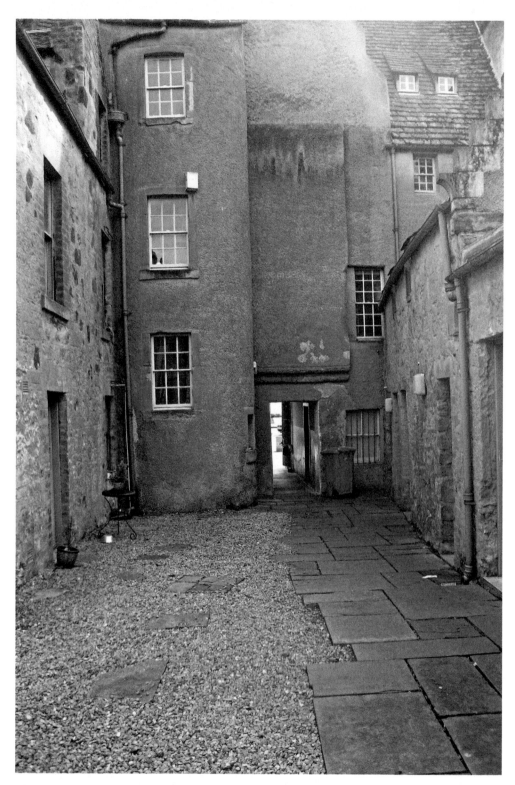

The rear view of Law's Close, looking on to the Forth.

'Well well,' I said, 'I can't help it and must do as I am told I suppose – when do we start and where are you going to send us? Take off your liquor quick and be hanged to you, you are a pretty set of blackguards to be sure – wait till I get you in Kirkcaldy and you'll catch it.' Next day we all had to leave the ship on our road to a small village near Moscow, nearly 400 miles from St Petersburg. We went off bag and baggage escorted by some Russian officers and poor creatures of soldiers, the crew walking and I riding on a small Russian pony. We were fed and allowed a few copecks (less than a penny) to the man and rouble to me a day. When the officer offered me the money, I told him to keep it as he needed it more than me.

'After a good deal of hardships passing through the small Russian villages on the way, we came at last to the Moscow district where we were billeted in a small town on the river Mosova. The people were kind to us as far as they could, and I was allowed to walk about; I got acquainted with one of the magistrates or governors of the district, and I used to go to his house and visit him and the family. The Russians are naturally a kind hearted and innocent people and so I found them but their priests keep them very strict and everything and every circumstance must be blessed.

'We had it very cold sometimes and many were frost bitten; it first appears on the cheek like a white mark and no pain, but the moment any friend sees it, he flies to you with snow in his hand and rubs your cheek hard till it disappears – I have seen it as low as 10 degrees below zero.

'They are happy creatures, how they dance and sing, and when winter is fairly set in and the snow gets hard, how splendidly the fellows thunder along on their sledges. The Russians are great dancers and sing well too. However when an order came for so many to be drawn for the army, what a sad commotion it made, women and girls crying. They were drawn by lot and all the unlucky fellows were soon bundled off, never in all likelihood to return.

'One day at the beginning of spring I called over to see my friend the Governor who looked curious and sad; he exclaimed "Oh Captain Oliphant, have you heard the sad news?" (I thought in my own mind, what can he mean, has Paul ordered us all to Siberia?) "I am grieved to tell you, Captain, our beloved Czar Paul is gone." "Gone, where is he gone to, does no-one know where he is?" "Oh Captain, Captain, he is dead; one of the Russian Courier officers brought me word yesterday, our beloved Czar took ill and died suddenly." "Well well, it can't be helped," I said, "however Governor I'm very sorry for it, but what will we do now?" He said nothing so I went back pretending to be sorry, while inwardly hoping that this might be the means of freeing us from our captivity, and so it proved.'

In 1837 Mary, another member of the Oliphant family, married Robert Hutchison who took over the East Bridge Mill, then (as again shown on the 1824 map) a distillery belonging to Spears & Company. It seems that her family were initially not all that happy with the match: but Robert went on to replace the distillery with his own Hutchison's flour mill, which still operates today although under different ownership. The fine Georgian house at the foot of the Path was built in the 1750s and is still used as the offices of the flour mill.

Another sixteenth-century house, now category A Listed and originally built for David Law, a wealthy merchant and shipowner, is Law's Close (sometimes known now as the Merchant's House) at 339 High Street at the east end of Kirkcaldy. It had fallen into disrepair and was latterly a tenement housing several families with shops on the ground floor. Local people can still remember when the shops on street level included a fish and chip shop and a small (and very dark) branch Post Office. The building was saved from dereliction and almost certain demolition by the Scottish Historic Buildings Trust, which became involved in the 1980s, purchasing most of the house in 1986 and by 1996 owning the whole property, having raised funds to restore and save the building for posterity. The restoration project consisted of several phases, which took twenty years in total to complete and included archaeological investigations and historic research that identified different building phases, important features and some quite unique details, all of which were recorded. Importantly, while the building has been sensitively repaired, it has not been over-restored: some of the original woodwork has been retained in its original state, and in some cases a section of the old wood has been left in the middle of the new panelling.

The first floor originally consisted of a central hall with a large fireplace in the centre, with a room leading off it on each side. The walls were plastered with lime and the ceilings

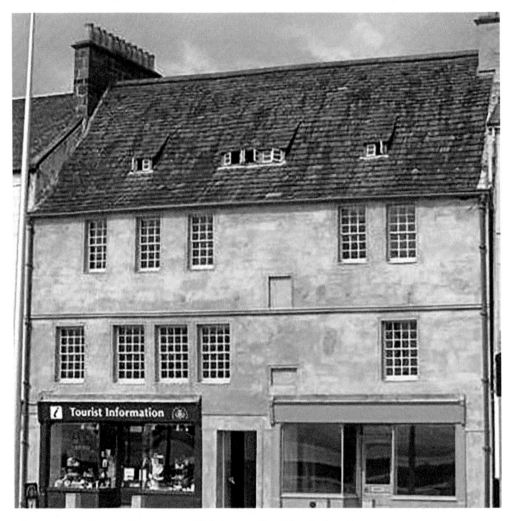

The exterior of Law's Close on the High Street. (Paul Zander)

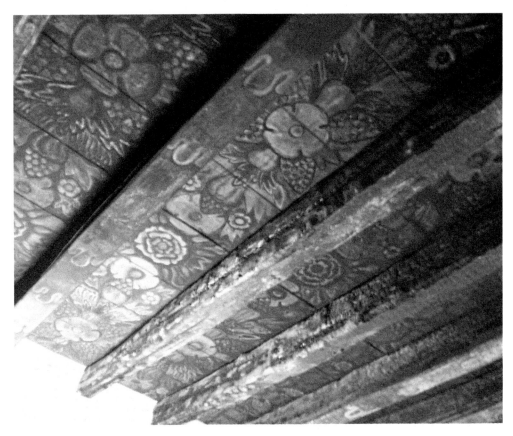

The ancient ceiling beams, decorated with flowers and fruit, have been carefully preserved in one of the rooms in Law's Close.

of the main rooms were actually the wooden boards and joists of the floor above, which had been painted with patterns of fruit, leaves and geometric figures. By about 1670, to keep up with the fashions of the times, the interior was changed to wood panelling on the walls and decorative plaster on the ceilings.

Among the fine original features that have been uncovered and preserved there are sixteenth-century painted ceilings and a late seventeenth-century plaster ceiling. The original plaster mouldings with fruit, foliage and figures have been brought back as near to their original condition as possible without damaging the fabric of the building. Traces of the Kirkcaldy burgh arms, painted in black distemper, were also discovered on the east wall, and ceiling beams painted with fruit and flowers were also uncovered. Remarkably, an early mural of a sailing ship, possibly commemorating the arrival of Anne of Denmark to Kirkcaldy in 1589, can still be seen on one wall. Standing at the front windows today, there is still a clear view of the harbour and it is easy to imagine a shipowner looking across to keep track of his shipping. The building is now used as office premises with a well designed and landscaped long rigg garden at the rear, which is looked after by enthusiastic volunteers. Law's Close was officially opened to the public in 2005 by the former Prime Minister Gordon Brown and a plaque has been placed on the exterior by the Historic Buildings Trust and Kirkcaldy Civic Society.

The early nineteenth-century Harbour House at 427 High Street was possibly also owned by William Oliphant, as its elevated position gives an excellent view of the harbour and the shipping traffic. A fine three-storey building topped by a distinctive pediment, it had fallen into disrepair and was used as a lodging house with multiple occupancy and very poor facilities. It too was rescued from dereliction as part of Kirkcaldy's Townscape Heritage Initiative and converted into individual flats for Viewpoint Housing Association. The major renovation included demolishing all the internal floors, walls and roof and completely recreating the interior to make it once again a handsome building.

Not all the shipowners chose to live at the harbour. George Elder, merchant and owner of the schooner *Minerva*, his wife Joanna and their four sons lived in a splendid mansion called Adelaide House on the site where the present Town House now stands, as well as having business premises opposite the harbour. In 1839 the family started to extend their business interests to South Australia, and his second eldest son Alexander sailed on *Minerva* with a large and varied cargo including agricultural machinery, seeds, rum, gunpowder and biscuits. He later expanded his business interests by buying up land and acting as agents for shipping companies. He was joined in Australia later by his brother William and William's wife (whose maiden name was Malcolm, presumably a member of another ship-owning family), and then by his other two brothers, George and Thomas. The young men must have established strong business interests, as Elders Ltd still have a huge flourishing agriculture business in Australia today. Whether Elder chose to re-name his home Adelaide House after his sons set up in business in Australia, or whether it was the original name which sparked off their interests there, can only be conjectured.

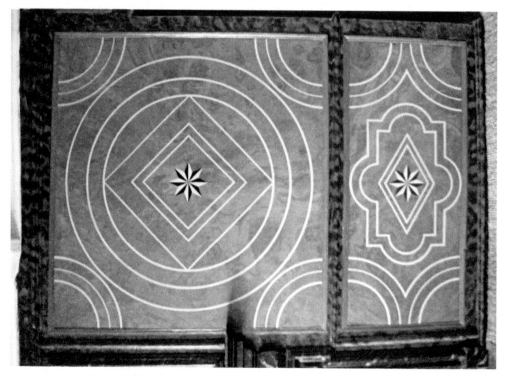

A section of the beautiful panelling in Law's Close.

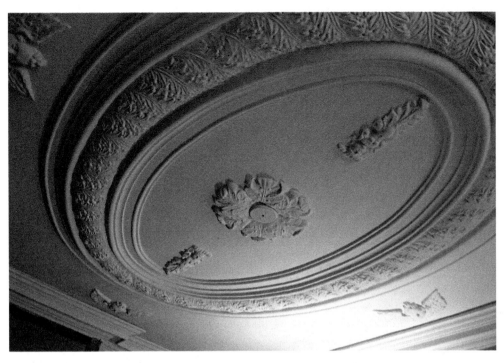

An ornate plaster ceiling in Law's Close has been carefully restored.

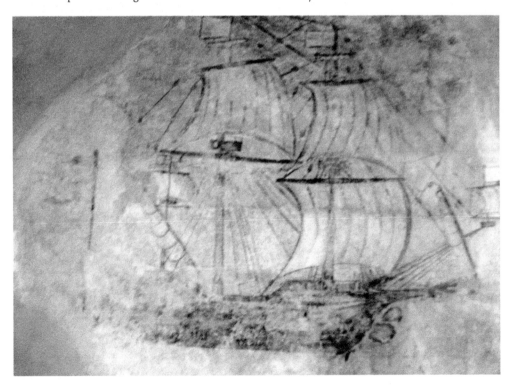

This faded seventeenth-century wall painting of a sailing ship can still be made out in one room of Law's Close.

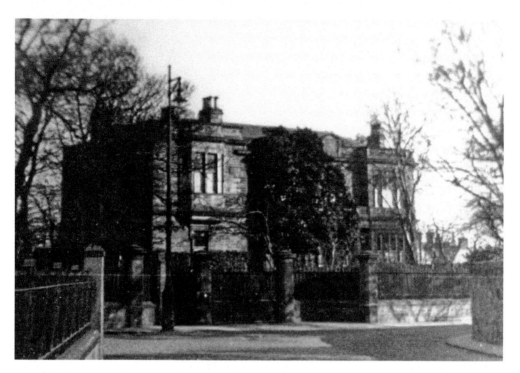

Adelaide House was the home of the wealthy shipowning Elder family. (Kirkcaldy Civic Society)

CHAPTER 5

Imports and Exports

Kirkcaldy harbour has had a long history of importing goods and exporting manufactured items: even by the end of the seventeenth century there were fourteen vessels in coal trade with Holland and London. Although most of the goods carried were utilitarian, a record from 1619 shows the Kirkcaldy ship *Jennet* was carrying hatbands embroidered in gold and silver. Timber came in from Baltic ports and Kirkcaldy was the landing port for the timber for Falkland Palace.

By the end of the seventeenth century, Kirkcaldy had fourteen ships trading to and from Holland. As early as 1752, Captain George Baker is recorded as taking his ship *Martha and Mary* to and from the Baltic ports, with cargoes including 3 tons of Swedish iron

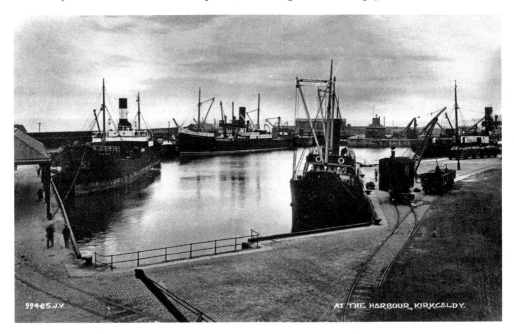

A typically busy scene at Kirkcaldy harbour in the 1950s and 1960s, including a Coast Line cement ship with chevron on the funnel.

from Gothenburg for the nail makers of Pathhead. Sir John Oswald of Dunnikier (then MP for Kirkcaldy, and a wealthy and very influential landowner) is recorded as building up the local salt industry by improving the semicircular series of rocks called the Bucket Pats, which collected the salt water. It was then pumped into the adjacent salt pans and converted into salt by evaporation. Kirkcaldy had an enormous trade in salt with the Continent, and in the early eighteenth century export and import duties amounted to well over £5,000; but this trade collapsed with the discovery of mineral rock salt from Germany.

However, the early records of Kirkcaldy Burgh had some stern words to warn against smuggling: 'The Council, from its own experience, is convinced that the smuggling of brandy, tea and other foreign commodities is pernicious and destructive to the good of the county. Therefore it is determined to discourage as far as its own powers are available to stop all smuggling of foreign goods of whatever category.' There was also concern for the welfare of local manufacturers; in 1740 for instance it was decided that yarn should be free of customs duty 'for all time coming'.

At one time a large amount of flax was grown in Fife for the local linen mills: in 1854 for instance, 1,648 acres of flax had been sown across the county. An early report in the 1850s stated: 'On going through the countryside in Fife in those days one could see the delicate blue bells dangling in the fields, and the carts with flax travelling to the lint mills.' But by 1857 flax was not mentioned in the Agricultural Reports, and it was obvious that farmers had started to cultivate other, presumably more profitable, crops. Ten years later there was an effort to revive the industry, and 109 acres of flax were grown; but from 1890 to 1918 the growing of flax locally practically stopped altogether.

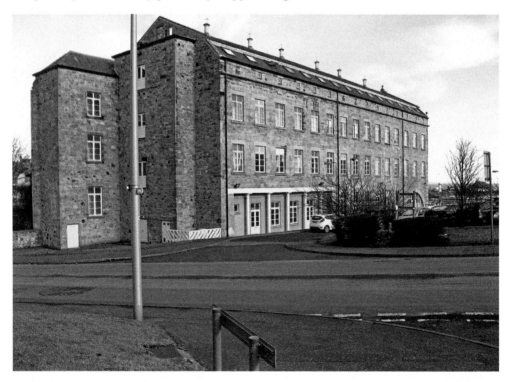

The West spinning mill used flax in its linen manufacture.

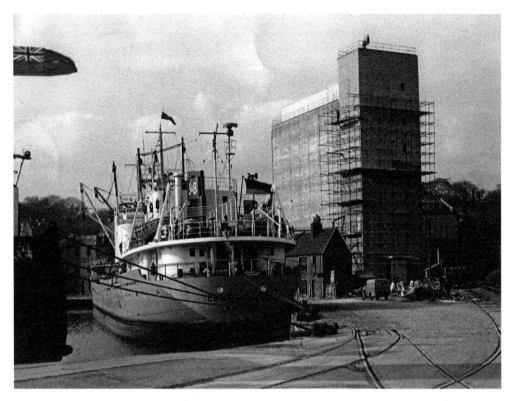

Elise Schulte was one of the huge ships to transport grain in the 1950s to what was then Hutchison's flour mill. (Tom Mutch)

As the linen mills were still prospering, flax had to be imported. A huge amount of both flax and jute came in from Russia, and the steamer *Danube* came in from Archangel in 1869 with what was thought to be the largest cargo of jute ever carried in a single ship. In 1870 it was reported that the quantity of flax imported at Kirkcaldy over five years averaged over 4,000 tons, which was a huge amount. The imports from Russia continued over many years, as well as coming from the Baltic States, France, Belgium and Holland. During the First World War, owing to the difficulty of getting supplies from Russia, local production started up again, and in 1919 more than 1,000 acres of flax were sown across Fife. After the Second World War there were still reports of it being imported, mainly from Belgium and Holland, with small quantities coming from New Zealand, Australia, Canada and Egypt.

There must have been quite a stir when Provost Swan drove on to the harbour in his smart landau and a pair of horses with his friend Thomas Carlyle (who taught in Kirkcaldy Burgh School from 1816 to 1818) by his side. Carlyle's post was secured when Provost Swan

strongly recommended a Mr Carlyle who since his arrival in town had been examined on general requirements by the Minister, who wrote that there is no doubt that his education in classical literature has been thorough and complete. There are few young men of his standing who have directed their studies to a greater variety of subjects or had displayed a more extensive range of knowledge.

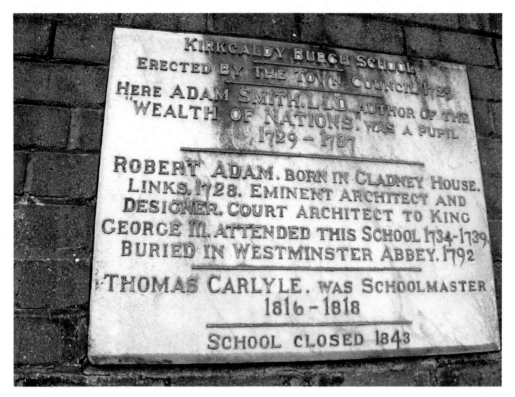

KIRKCALDY BURGH SCHOOL
ERECTED BY THE TOWN COUNCIL 1725
HERE ADAM SMITH. LL.D. AUTHOR OF THE
WEALTH OF NATIONS. WAS A PUPIL
1729 – 1737

ROBERT ADAM. BORN IN GLADNEY HOUSE.
LINKS. 1728. EMINENT ARCHITECT AND
DESIGNER. COURT ARCHITECT TO KING
GEORGE III. ATTENDED THIS SCHOOL 1734-1739
BURIED IN WESTMINSTER ABBEY. 1792

THOMAS CARLYLE. WAS SCHOOLMASTER
1816 – 1818

SCHOOL CLOSED 1843

This plaque in Hill Street marks the site of Carlyle's school.

At the time there were two German ships in the dock discharging bales of flax, which was something of great interest to the Provost, who owned a large linen company. The old records report: 'Provost Swan walked over to talk to his cargo receiver and examined the flax, pulling out strand after strand to test it for length and pliability of fibre. Carlyle watched with great interest and nodded his head as if to say "Well well, you are a good business man" – as indeed he was.'

Carlyle also recorded:

Kirkcaldy itself had many looms as well as Baltic trade and whale fishing. Its flax mill machinery, I remember, was turned mainly by wind and curious blue painted wheels with oblique vanes rising from many roofs – though how working I never saw. The Kirkcaldy population were a pleasant collection of honest fellow mortals with something of the faithfulness of good old Scotch in their works and ways.

The town must have made a good impression on Carlyle, as he recalled: 'The beach of Kirkcaldy in summer twilight, a mile of the smoothest sand with one long wave coming on gently, steadily and breaking into a gradual explosion; beautiful sounding and advancing, ran from south to north from west burn to Kirkcaldy harbour – a favourite scene and beautiful to me still in a far off way.'

By the 1800s, the town had exports of its own with its linoleum, other floor coverings and various manufactured goods, with weekly sailings to London, Hull, Liverpool and Bristol.

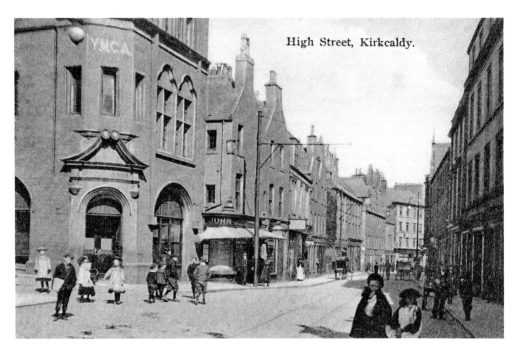

High Street, Kirkcaldy.

The Provost Swan Memorial Building still stands at the foot of Kirk Wynd.

Once the harbour was improved in 1846, shipping improved with it: Kirkcaldy-owned ships were trading to North and South America, France, the Mediterranean and the Baltic. Foreign ships came in from Norway, Denmark and Germany and it was estimated that an average of ninety-two ships came in yearly with flax, timber and other cargoes. In 1849 Lockhart's *Adam Smith* was advertised in the *Fifeshire Advertiser* as having 'arrived direct from Peru with a cargo of Peruvian guano'; and in the same paper, R. Hutchison & Sons advertised the expected arrival of a similar cargo.

When the whalers stopped in the nineteenth century, their vacant berths were occupied in the 1860s and 1870s by ships such as *Triad, Falcon, Kohinoor* and *George Ann,* all belonging to Swan Brothers and taking part in the flax trade to Baltic ports in the summer while spending the winter bringing sugar from the West Indies to Greenock. This sugar trade in the 1870s was carried out by a large number of vessels, and one of the fastest voyages on the run was completed by the Dysart-built barque *Lothrie* in the record time of four weeks. By 1890 this trade too fell away and these ships were all sold.

Imports and exports were wide and varied, reflecting the nature of the town's industries. The local potteries, for instance, used the harbour for imports of some of their raw materials and exports of their earthenware. In the 1830s, Methven's pottery in the Links area of Kirkcaldy is recorded as exporting crates of earthenware to Dundee, as well as sending numerous casks of old iron and bags of rags to Glasgow, London and Newcastle. The firm also imported flint stone, red and white lead, and glass, mainly from Newcastle, to use in their manufacture. Fife Pottery in the Gallatown also had a thriving market, sending goods, especially teapots, to Ireland; the Irish cargoes were easily recognisable as they were sent in crates made by their own workers and packed in wood shavings instead of straw for public health reasons.

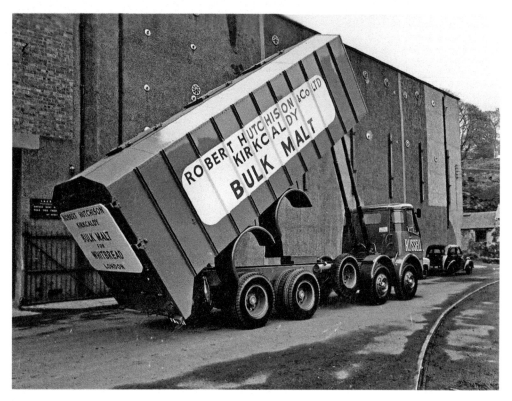

One of the heavy-duty lorries belonging to Robert Hutchison delivering malt to the mill. (Tom Mutch)

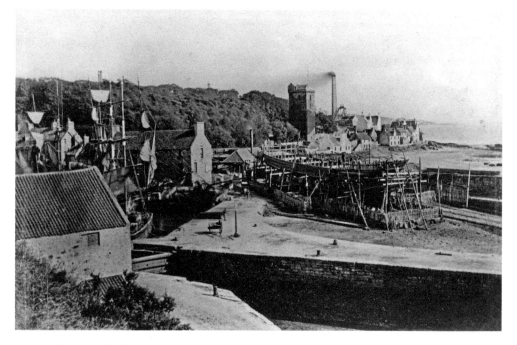

Dysart shipyard, which built the barque *Lothrie*. (Dysart Trust)

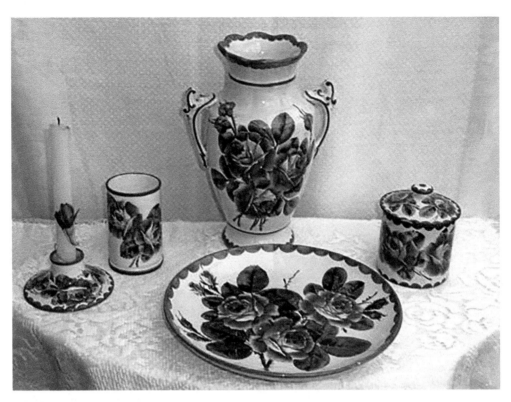

Abbotsford pottery would be exported from the harbour. (George Hunter)

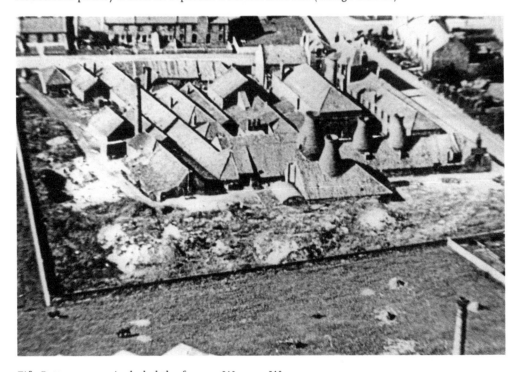

Fife Pottery wares included the famous Wemyss Ware.

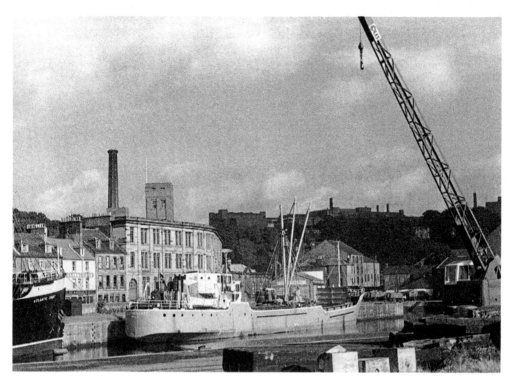

Nairn's canvas factory was built right opposite the harbour. (Kirkcaldy Galleries)

Ravenscraig Chemical Works, which were situated near Nairn's first factory on Pathhead Sands, manufactured pitch in the 1850s; around 300 tons of this was exported in barrels to France and Spain. Tobacco too was imported, with the last cargo of tobacco being brought in huge drums in 1908. In 1910 SS *Ravenscraig* and SS *Rosyth*, distinguished by their white funnels and black tops, were used in the Hull and Newcastle trades importing oils, paints, gum, chemicals and resin for the linoleum trade.

In the earlier years, the greater proportion of coal extracted from the Fife pits was used for local consumption, but in the nineteenth and early twentieth centuries, coal was exported from several Fife ports, including Kirkcaldy, Dysart and Burntisland, with Methil being the most prolific. Local pits such as the Frances Colliery in Dysart sent coal to ports in the Netherlands, Germany and Belgium. It was brought in by the lorry-load and transferred by conveyor belt straight into the holds of the ships waiting in the harbour. However, when Methil Docks expanded in 1913 to become the greatest coal exporting port in Scotland, shipping over 3 million tons of coal annually from three docks to ports all over the world, the coal transport from Kirkcaldy harbour reduced considerably. The outbreak of the First World War meant that the amount of coal cargoes decreased dramatically, with the total shipments throughout Fife amounting to 16,000 tons in 1914, compared to 131,000 tons for the corresponding week in the previous year.

The early years of the twentieth century started to show cause for concern in the harbour trade. P. K. Livingstone, in his book *A History of Kirkcaldy* (1843–1949), pointed out that over the forty-four years from 1905 to 1948, there were only six years that showed a profit on the working of the harbour.

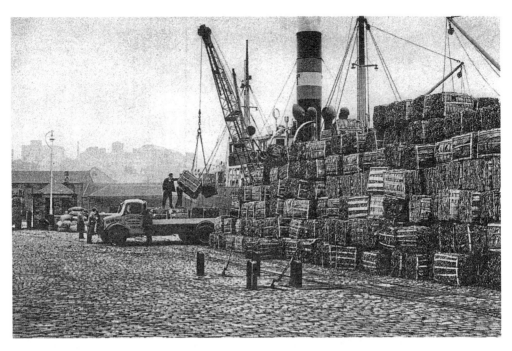

A shipment of cork for the linoleum trade. (Kirkcaldy Civic Society)

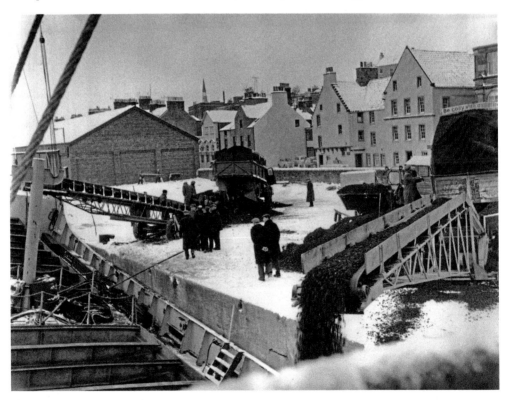

Coal was delivered from local collieries and tipped directly onto the ships by conveyor belts. (Kirkcaldy Civic Society)

This was partly due to heavy debt charges which will continue, assuming no further capital expenditure arises, until May 1979. The harbour would be self supporting but for annual sums required to meet debt liquidation and loan interest.

During the First World War the dock was taken over by the American Navy as a naval base and was more or less closed to shipping. In the Second World War regular services were maintained with difficulty; however the Ministry of Food directed a stated quantity of seed potatoes to the coasting trade, so for six years from 1942 there was considerable traffic in potatoes to Newcastle, Hull, London and Liverpool.

Records for the three years ending May 1938 showed the highest gross earnings in the history of the harbour, with regular sailings to and from London, Hull, Liverpool and Bristol. Imports amounted to 112,000 tons and exports to 63,397 tons. The main classes of cargo imported were (in tonnage): cement 31,810, linseed oil 9,466, cork 18,077, whiting 10,095 and chemicals 6,953. Although the export trade in coal had stopped for the time being, there were still considerable exports (again in tonnage) in linoleum 33,959, paper 12,786, malt 3,283, and potatoes 1,830.

It's apparent then that one of the largest industries to utilise the harbour was the linoleum trade, with Nairn's and Barry, Ostlere & Shepherd having several large factories in the town. Bales of cork were imported from Portugal, Spain and North Africa and were distributed not just within Kirkcaldy but also to factories in Newburgh and Falkland, and were included in the manufacture of huge quantities of rolls of linoleum, which were exported virtually worldwide.

The building industry was another important factor in harbour trade as it depended on the regular Coast Line ships to bring in their vital cement. In the second half of the twentieth century, there were six builders' merchants' premises lining the harbour:

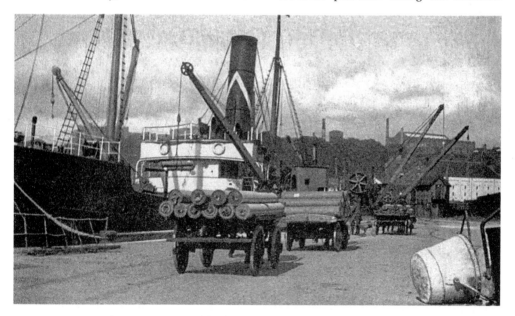

The linoleum industry was a major user of the harbour, with direct access allowing them to ship huge amounts of rolls of linoleum virtually worldwide.

Johnson & Paton, Lawson, Currie & Company, McCreath Taylor, Monteith Building Services and Henderson. When the cement ships, such as the *Welsh Coast, British Coast* and *Atlantic Coast,* came in, all easily distinguished by the white chevron on their funnels, the harbour immediately became a hive of activity. The local premises of the Dundee, Perth & London Shipping Company were just across the road, and DP&LS manager Watson Dingwall assigned each incoming cargo to the relevant merchant. One of the earlier cement ships, *Carmarthen Coast,* was tragically sunk by a mine in November 1939.

To facilitate freight transport, a single-track branch railway line was installed in 1848, running from Kirkcaldy station to the harbour, crossing the Path by bridge. This line, a branch of the North British Railway, was exceptionally steep, having a gradient of 1:21. This was the main cause of not one but four spectacular accidents over the years when the locomotive and its wagons ran out of control and, on three out of the four occasions, ended up plunging into the water. The first accident was in April 1901, between 5 and 6 a.m., when the engine and its seven wagons, which were heavily laden with paper (probably from Tullis Russell's paper mill near Markinch), grain and potatoes, started the steep descent to the harbour. It was destined for shipment on the regular weekly sailing from Kirkcaldy to London, but it gathered speed so fast that the brakes lost their power and (according to bemused onlookers) sparks were seen flying from its wheels.

According to a report in the *Fife Free Press* on 13 April 1901:

The driver stuck to his post until the engine was a few yards from the pier, when with great presence of mind he succeeded in leaping from the rushing train and escaped without injury. The engine, along with three of its wagons, went over the edge of the pier

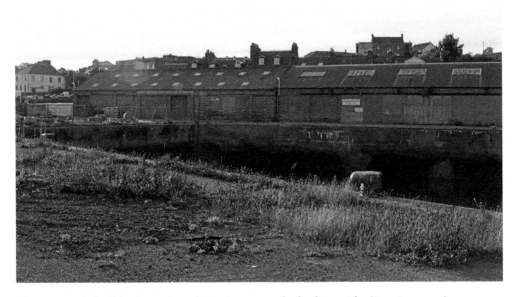

There were six builders' merchants' warehouses at the harbour side. (Don Swanson)

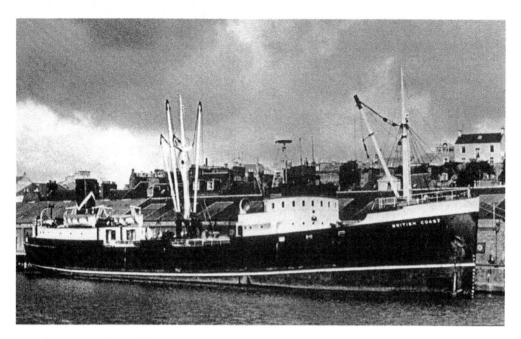

British Coast, another of the Coastline fleet, was a regular visitor to the harbour with products for the building trade. (Kirkcaldy Galleries)

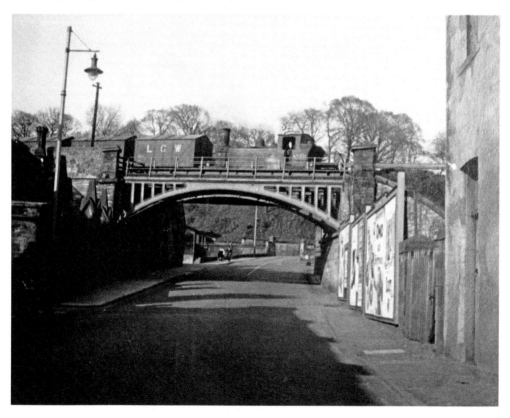

A single-track branch railway line to carry freight to the harbour crossed the Path by bridge.

and crashed into the water. There was a hiss of steam and all was quiet. The engine driver and a stevedore found the engine lying on its side on the sand below, on the top being a heavy goods van and an open wagon, while a third open wagon was in a suspended position against the front of the quay wall, with the trucks forming the rear of the train remaining on the quay.

A steam crane arrived from St Margaret's, a staff of workmen had a temporary line of rails laid to the end of the pier and the crane was soon at work: before night all the wagons had been hoisted up. The engine, estimated to weigh between 30 and 40 tons, was also embedded in the sand and it was found too heavy a lift for the crane. The next day a crane was brought from Cowlairs and operations were commenced to hoist the engine; the engine was got on to the pier and it was found it had escaped with comparatively slight damage.

Another incident in May 1910 saw the train running out of control and travelling 400 yards before striking the buffers, although on that occasion it did manage to keep on the rails. The driver, John Cowan, and his fireman, John McLauchlan, jumped clear with minor injuries.

The official North British Railway accident report said:

Cowan was the driver of a train which left Kirkcaldy for Kirkcaldy Harbour about 2.45 pm. The train consisted of a four wheeled tank engine, eight loaded mineral wagons, one loaded wagon and a brake truck. Shortly after the train had started, Cowan found

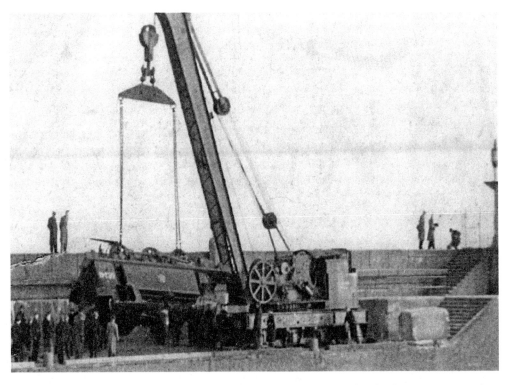

The small goods train ran out of control and crashed into the harbour on more than one occasion. (Kirkcaldy Civic Society)

that he was unable to keep it under proper control, and it entered the harbour lines at considerable speed.

The train travelled over the waterside line in the harbour, which is approximately level, for a distance of about four hundred yards, and the engine struck the buffer stops. Cowan jumped from the engine when it was about two hundred yards from the buffer stops, and strained the muscles of his left leg. His foreman, John McLaughlan, jumped from the engine later and was not injured. The buffer stops were displaced and the life guard bolts of the engine were damaged. William Reid, the guard of the train, was riding on the brake truck and was not injured.

In comparatively recent times, two similar accidents occurred in October 1942 and November 1954 – with the same driver, James Adamson, on both occasions. The most recent accident, which required the retrieval of the engine from the waters of the Forth, is still vividly remembered by the crowds of local people who flocked to the harbour to watch the recovery. In a newspaper interview at the time, Adamson recalled how the wheels of his engine locked as the train with sixteen carriages hurtled down the steep slope.

Willie [Millar, the twenty-one-year-old fireman] and I applied the sand brakes, but the gale was blowing the sand away before it reached the rail. I remembered what happened to me in 1942, and I realised it was happening all over again. When I realised it was hopeless, I told Willie 'It's time we were out of here' and after I jumped clear, I saw Willie lying on

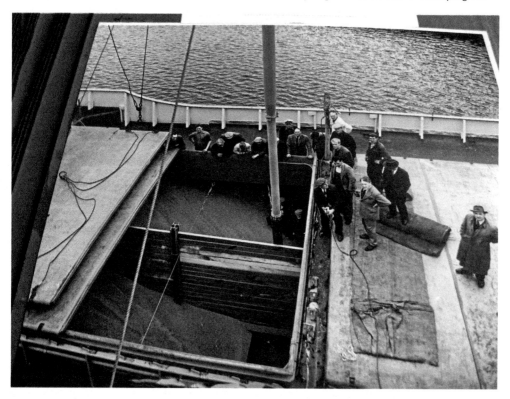

Grain for the flour mill being inspected in the hold in the 1950s. (Carr's Hutchison Mill)

the steps. He had hit his head on the concrete and was taken to hospital with a suspected fracture of his skull.

After I looked round I saw that the engine had gone. I never heard it falling. People asked me if I would go back to the job again – but I did, as I didn't see why I shouldn't go – car drivers go back after road accidents, don't they?

Another newspaper report described the rescue of the runaway engine under the heading 'A three-hour free Sunday show' – as crowds gathered at the harbour to watch the dripping engine being hauled out of the water. The engine lost its funnel and its tender was smashed, but the cabin from which the two men escaped was undamaged. The branch line was officially closed to traffic in October 1984.

A local man recalled: 'I remember when the first ship came in from the USSR around 1960 during the Cold War period, the *Artika* from Murmansk flying the hammer and sickle Soviet flag. That caused quite a stir round the harbour: I don't know what her cargo was, possibly flax, but the crew were not allowed to leave the ship to come ashore.'

A different incident – but still fondly remembered by all those who saw it in the early 1960s – was when a swordfish followed a foreign ship into the harbour and became trapped in the dock. One onlooker said:

It must have been about 10 feet long and kept swimming round and round. A ship had come in from warmer climes and it was thought that the crew of the ship had been throwing food into the water for the swordfish which kept following it. There had been no new ships coming in for two days so the dock gate had been kept closed until the men were told to leave the gate open. Then as the ship sailed from the dock, the crew started to throw out more food; the swordfish followed its fresh meal until it got back to the open waters and presumably into warmer climes.

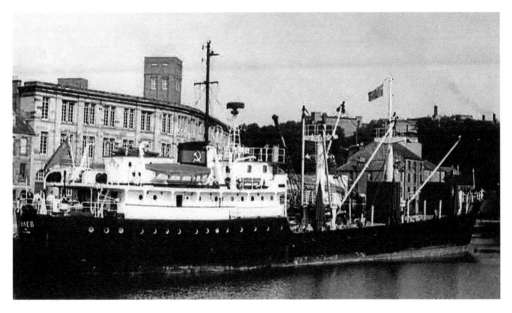

A ship from the USSR docked in the harbour around 1960. (Kirkcaldy Galleries)

CHAPTER 6

Present Day

Kirkcaldy harbour today looks very different from the bustling port of a hundred or even fifty years ago.

Gone now are the ships carrying cement, cork or coal, and the long line of builders' merchants set conveniently along the roadside. Gone too are the exploits of the public who used the harbour for their own enjoyment or training: many local people remember learning to swim for the first time at Kirkcaldy Amateur Swimming Club, which had been formed originally in 1886. The club first met at Seafield before moving to regular classes at the harbour basin, where it had its own small premises with dedicated trainers. 'Every

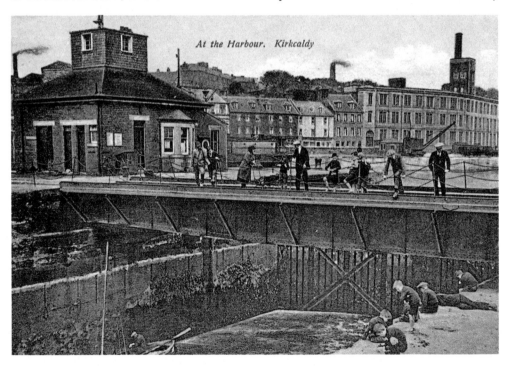

A branch railway handled commercial traffic.

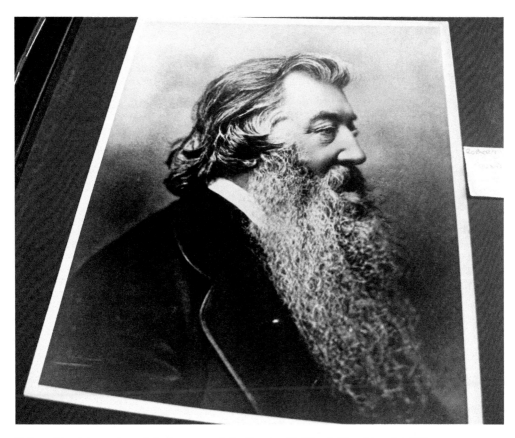

Robert Hutchison, the original owner of the flour mill. (Carr's Hutchison's Mill)

August there was a race from the harbour to the Tiel Burn and back – more than a mile each way,' recalled a local man. 'It was some swim – there was no actual prize, the prize was staying alive at the end of it!'

One local woman recalled swimming in the harbour many years ago when she and her friends were still at primary school. 'There were no premises for changing, but we just worked it that our friends would hold the towels round each other to preserve our decency. The water was awful as you can imagine, murky and greasy, but as it was before the first proper swimming pool was built it was where you went to learn to swim.'

One of the swimming galas, held in the basin in August 1938, drew a crowd of 3,000 to watch a varied programme of events including an 800-yard relay race for the Fife Coast Championship, which ended with a win for Kirkcaldy over Burntisland. The programme also featured a 25-yard Learners' Race, a crawl, dive and breaststroke race for the Rotary Shield, the McLelland Cup and the 200-yard relay race. The latter ended in disqualification as one of the swimmers failed to touch the post. It had to be re-run later at Buckhaven. During the interval, Mr Hunter, who was Fife Coast diving champion, gave an exhibition of swimming and diving, and the event ended with a water polo game, where the Whites beat the Blacks 2-0.

The club also hosted the Eastern District Long Distance Swim Championship in August 1956 when six hardy swimmers – four men and two women from clubs in Portobello, Leith

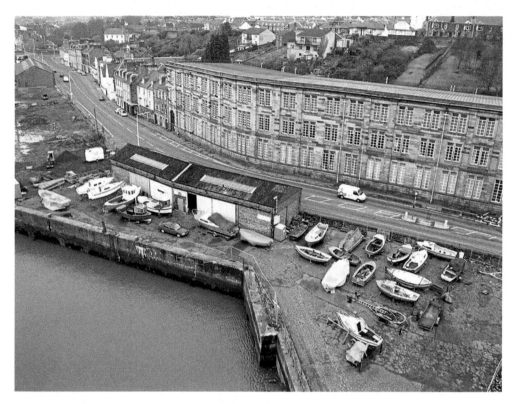

This aerial view of the harbour before the dockside housing development was built shows the facade of Nairn's canvas factory. (Don Swanson)

and Burntisland as well as Bill Dewar from Kirkcaldy – took part on a Saturday evening in a choppy sea and low water temperatures. The course was from the Prom steps towards Inchkeith for approximately 1½ miles and then inwards towards the shore parallel to the Esplanade, with the finish at the Port Brae steps. Despite the adverse conditions, only two competitors failed to finish the course, which was approximately 3 miles. An inter-club swimming gala was also staged that month in the harbour basin when Burntisland Swimming Club beat Kirkcaldy by 54 points to 41. The gala also included a water polo match, again won by Burntisland by two goals to one.

Kirkcaldy Sea Cadets had their own ship, an ex-trawler, where the boys were trained in various aspects of seamanship. Their expertise was put to a severe test on one occasion when a fierce summer storm increased to a sudden gale and blew the ship right out of the harbour and dashed it against the wall at the prom. A breaches-buoy was quickly brought to the scene and the boys were rescued one by one and taken back to dry land.

Meanwhile, the slowdown of commercial shipping was gradual but devastating, with several events contributing to the cause. The main reason was the decline of the town's industries, particularly the once flourishing linoleum trade, which formerly saw regular shipments of cork coming in and huge cargoes of rolls of linoleum leaving for different destinations, both within the UK and much further afield. The building industry saw a significant change when, after years of the Coast Line ships coming in with their dedicated cargoes of cement, Blue Circle in Dunbar started manufacturing its own cement in East

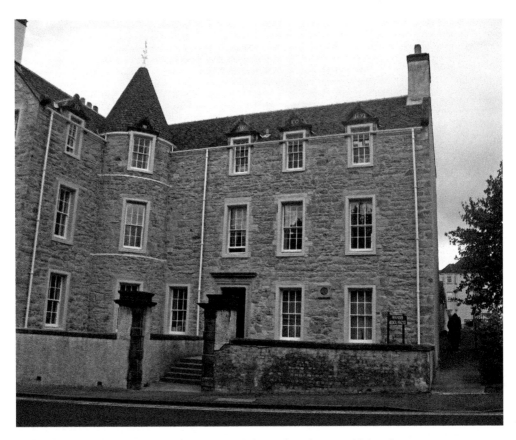

Path House, now beautifully restored, once belonged to the Oswald family.

Lothian. The opening of the Forth Road Bridge in September 1964 gave hauliers an attractive new option – to deliver their goods direct by road rather than by sea.

Thanks to the efforts of Kirkcaldy Civic Society, the structure of the harbour was awarded B Listed status in 1997. A distinctive small building known as the Harbourmaster's House at one time housed the mechanism for the railway bridge to swing open to let the ships through. Latterly, the building served as premises for the pilots who were on duty, particularly when foreign ships came in with their cargo and needed advice and directions to get over the mudbank outside the harbour mouth. The pilots, former merchant seamen, worked shifts and hoisted a series of flags to tell the captains whether the way was clear to come into port or whether they would have to wait in the Forth until they were told to proceed.

In December 1967 the Forth Harbour Reorganisation Scheme, constituting Forth Ports Authority, became law and was responsible for six ports grouped within the Firth of Forth, including Kirkcaldy, Methil and Burntisland.

As traffic slowed down and virtually stopped, the Forth Ports Authority (now Forth Ports Ltd) took over the ownership and operation of the harbour in 1967 from the then Kirkcaldy Town Council. With little or no commercial shipping coming in, the harbour started to silt up with mud and debris until this was dredged by Forth Ports, which now clears the inner basin annually, based on the amount of silt that has gathered, and the outer basin on a

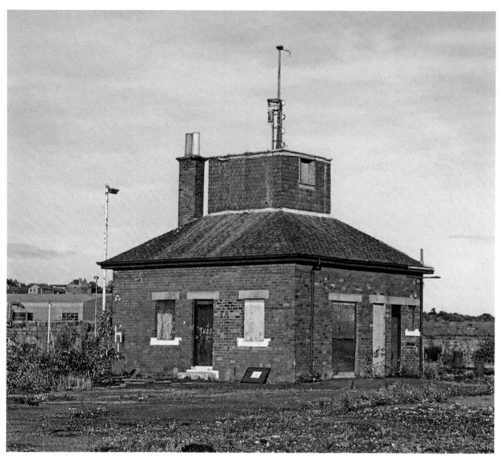

The small building originally housed the mechanism for the railway swing bridge. (Don Swanson)

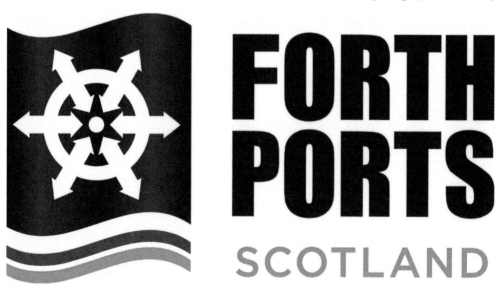

Forth Ports took over Kirkcaldy harbour in 1967. (Forth Ports Ltd)

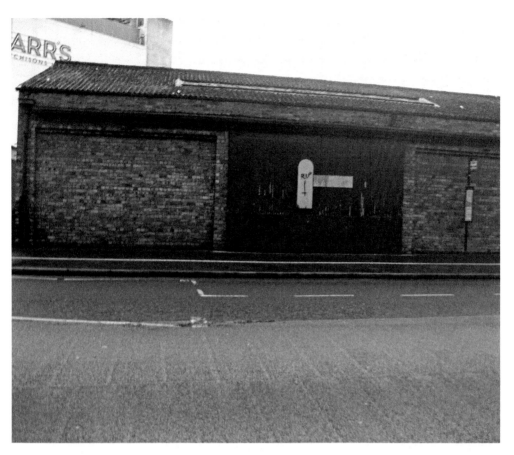

There is now only one left of the six builders' merchants' warehouses that bordered the harbour.

variable time scale. All but one of the builders' merchants' warehouses on the harbour side were demolished.

In 1998, plans were approved for a large estate of new housing to be built around the outer and inner harbour basin. The first phase was built in 2003 by Miller Homes and some years later a second phase of housing was completed by Penman Homes. One of the streets was named Lord Gambier Wharf in reference to one of Kirkcaldy's nineteenth-century whaling ships.

The old Harbourmaster's House came into use again briefly as it held the layout and description of the development, so that prospective buyers of the flats could see what was available from the plans. At the time it must have looked as if the harbour's only role was now to provide housing for the town, with little or no shipping apart from small leisure craft operated by Kirkcaldy Boat Club.

However, the tide – almost literally – began to turn when Carr's took over Hutchison's flour mill at the foot of the Path. Between 2010 and 2011 the company undertook a massive investment and by the following year a huge building, modernisation and reorganisation programme began. A new state-of-the-art mill and giant silos were built and some of the adjacent old buildings, now redundant, were demolished and the new complex was opened on site in 2013.

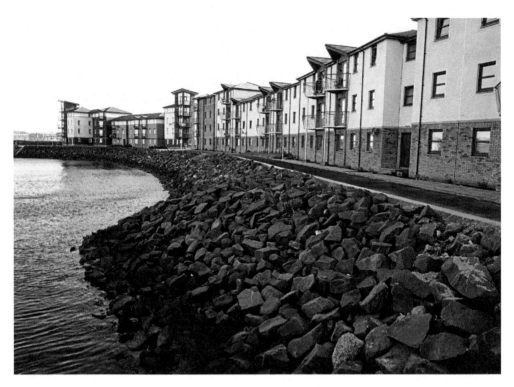

The new development of houses being built round the harbour. (Don Swanson)

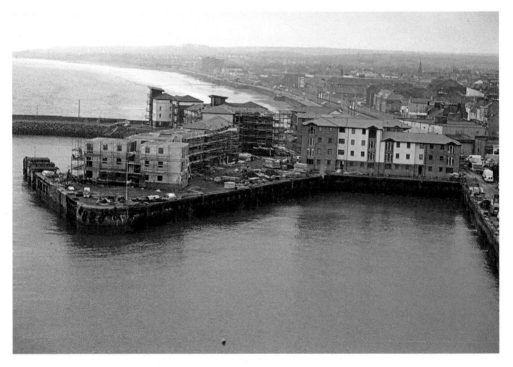

The large housing development started in 2003 and was built round the harbour area in two phases. (Don Swanson)

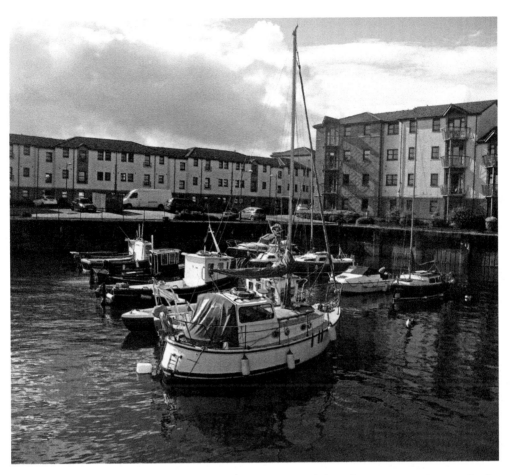

The small craft belonging to members of Kirkcaldy Boat Club make a picturesque scene in the water.

The company had previously been using Perth harbour but it was decided to investigate the possibilities of Kirkcaldy harbour being re-opened. Although by 1999 it was virtually disused by commercial shipping, the harbour had never been formally closed; this was in fact a great advantage, as if it had been closed it would have needed an Act of Parliament to re-open it. The only other viable option at the time was Burntisland harbour, but Carr's appreciation of the convenience of having Kirkcaldy harbour open again brought about the desired result. The harbour was again dredged by Forth Ports Ltd to clear the badly silted channel, enabling the grain ships to come in with their huge cargoes of wheat from home and abroad, including specialist varieties from mainland Europe, Canada and the USA.

The first ship to come in to the re-opened harbour was the *Danica Hav* in June 2011. Now Carr's have between forty and fifty ships a year coming in to Kirkcaldy harbour virtually all the year round. Much of the grain for bread production comes in from the South Coast, including East Sussex, Ridham in Kent, Dover and the Isle of Wight, as well as from parts of Europe. Flour from wheat grown locally across Fife comes in by road by large truck loads, although gone are the days when lorries at harvest time often had

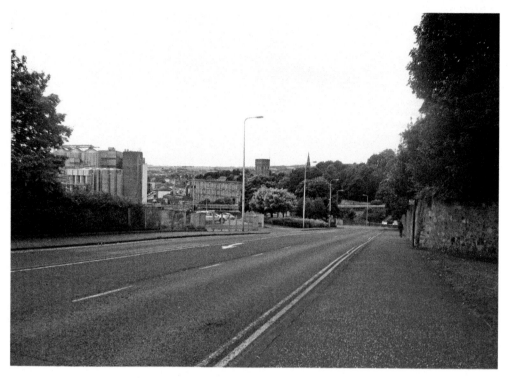

A view of Carr's premises from the top of the Path.

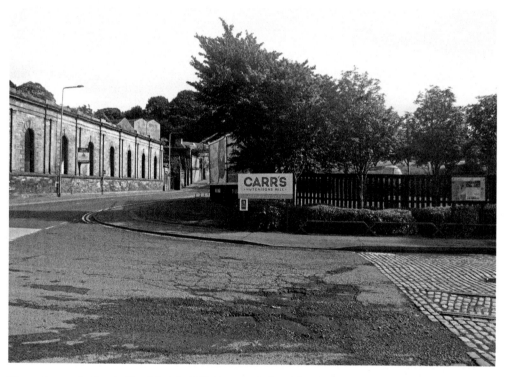

The entrance to Carr's Hutchison's Mill. Traces of the old railway track are still visible.

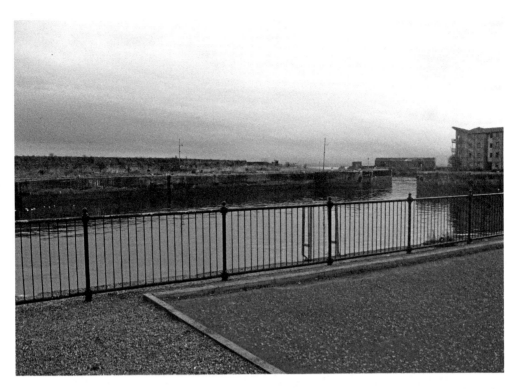

The former dock gates.

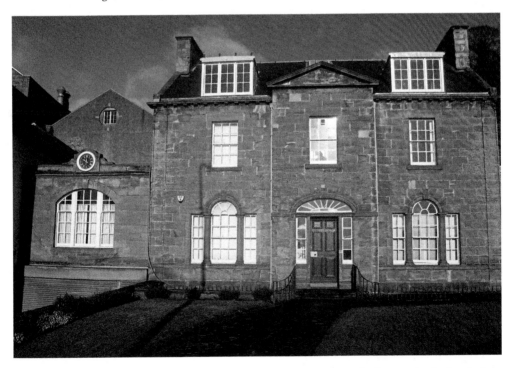

Carr's offices are situated in this beautiful Georgian house, which was built for Robert Hutchison, the original owner of the flour mill.

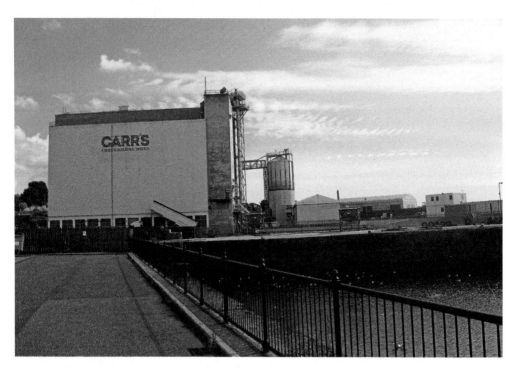

Carr's Hutchison's flour mill.

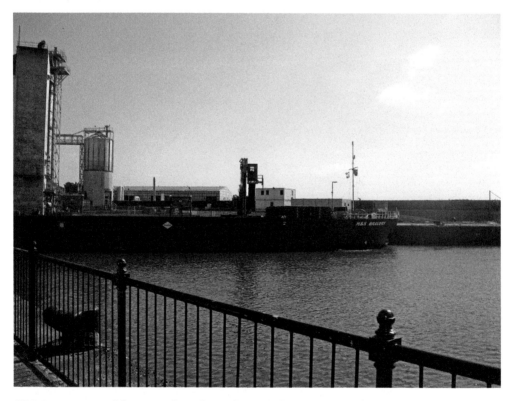

H&S Bravery, one of the grain ships that call regularly at the flour mill.

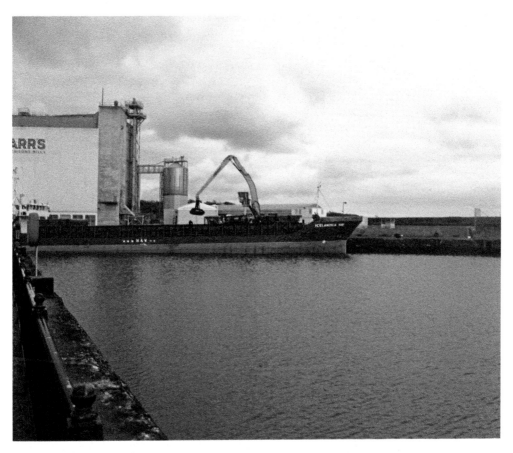

Icelandica Hav at Carr's flour mill.

to queue up on the Prom to wait their turn before their loads were siphoned out into the mill. The locally grown grain is still regarded as a key ingredient for biscuits and shortbread.

In most instances, the grain suppliers charter the ships to take the cargoes to the flour mill, bearing in mind that the ships must be a maximum of 87 metres long to be suitable for mooring at Kirkcaldy harbour. As Kirkcaldy is tidal, with two high and two low tides every 24 hours, the ships come in on the high tides each month, with around four or five ships coming in every month. Once each ship has been confirmed as suitable for the restrictions of the port, the shipping agent co-ordinates the date and time of its movements and notifies both Carr's and Forth Ports to ensure that the whole operation goes smoothly.

The long, low grain ships, such as *Sea Kestrel*, *Frisian River*, *Shetland Trader*, *Icelandica Hav* and *Sea Ruby*, are manoeuvred with expertise into the harbour by Forth Ports' pilots, who board and disembark at the small vessel anchorage south-east of Kirkcaldy known as Kirkcaldy Roads. While the ship's Master has the ultimate responsibility in principle for the safety of his ship, in practice it is often the pilot who takes the ship in on the Master's behalf. The whole process from when the pilot comes on board to berth the ship takes about 45 minutes, and the same time on departure when the pilot turns

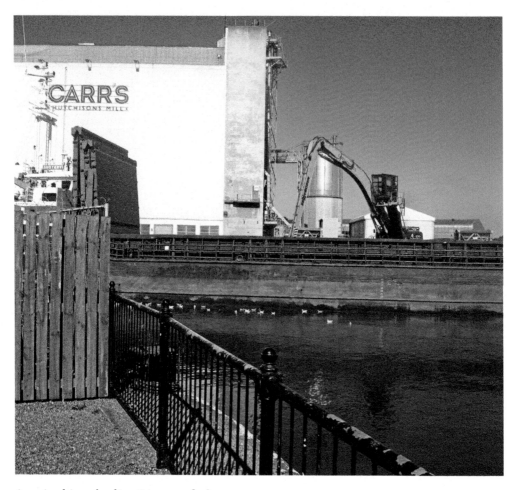

A grain ship unloading its cargo of wheat.

the ship back with the bow at the front and heads through the former dock gates back into the Forth again.

The shiploads of grain are efficiently scooped up by Forth Ports' cranes and deposited straight into the huge silos on the quayside. The latest technology is used for wheat cleaning, food safety, atmosphere control, blending and on-line quality control. The finished product is then delivered to manufacturers country-wide to be converted into bakery products that are enjoyed the world over, as the company now supplies all types of business from small and independent bakers to retail multiples and major food retailers.

It may be hundreds of years since Kirkcaldy harbour was once temporary home to the ships of James V, but its survival over the centuries in all its different stages and uses is a heartening prospect for the years to come.

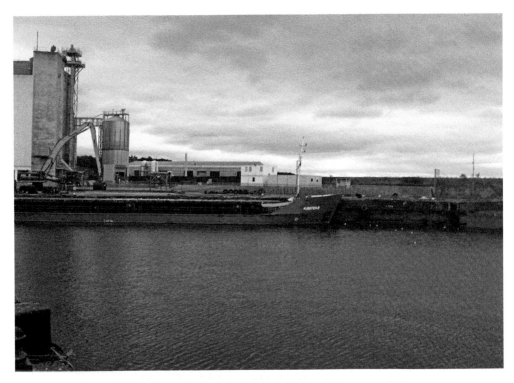

Kirsten B with a crane from Forth Ports Ltd scooping grain from the hold.

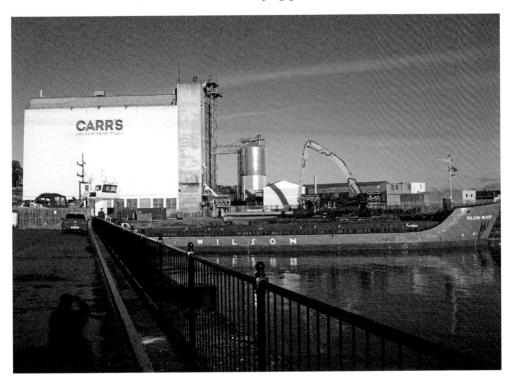

Grain ship *Wilson Weber* at the harbour.

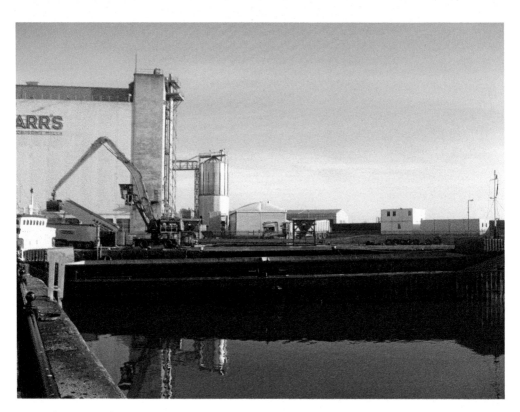

Grain ship *Sea Ruby* at Carr's mill.